Useful Baskets

Useful Baskets

BY MARA CARY   Houghton Mifflin Company   Boston   1977

By Mara Cary

Basic Baskets
Useful Baskets

Copyright © 1977 by Mara Cary

Library of Congress Cataloging in Publication Data

Cary, Mara.
  Useful baskets.

  Bibliography: p.
  1. Basket making. I. Title.
TT879.B3C38   746.4′1   77-22381
ISBN 0-395-25707-7   ISBN: 0-395-25950-9 pbk.

Printed in the United States of America

A 10 9 8 7 6 5 4 3 2 1

The poem on page vii is reprinted with the permission of the Bureau of American Ethnology of the Smithsonian Institution, *35th Annual Report*, 1921.

TO DICK AND DONICK

With Songs in My Pockets

To the Cedar Tree

Look at me, friend!
I come to ask for your dress . . .

I come to beg you for this,
Long-life Maker,
For I am going to make a basket for
   lily roots out of you.
I pray you, friend, not to feel angry . . .

Kwakiutl

THANKS   Ever and still to Andy and Bill. To my
teachers and my students: T.M., Gretchen Anderson,
Sam and Jane Kasten, Karen Borchert, Larry and Kathy Cronin,
Jon Aaron and Leslie Linsley, Dorothy Decker, Holly Brenizer,
David Marshall Brenizer, Shelby Stancioff, Sally Carter,
Judy Currie, Morgen Dietrich Van Voorst, Ginny Cianciolo,
Maida Fishman, Terry Rostov, Carol Hart, Ed Rossbach,
Virginia Harvey, Gloria Roth Teleki, Osma Tod,
George Wharton James, Frances Tenenbaum, and
Harriet Carter.

Contents

Easiest Basket, Tea Strainer, Pencil
Basket, Gretchen's Basket, Sewing Basket,
Scrap Basket, Laundry Basket, Little
Things Basket, Covered Bottles, Planters,
Onion Storage Basket, Hamper, Fruit
Basket, Lettuce Washer, Silverware Holders,
Berry Basket, Hat, Doll's Chair and Table,
Casserole Basket, Lamp, Soft Carriers

Foreword

Here is Mara Cary's second book on basket making. The first was published in 1975 and is called *Basic Baskets*. And it is just what the title implies, an excellent how-to-do-it book on basket making. Many people have told me with delight that they have made a basket or several baskets by following the instructions in the first book. But then, their interest stimulated, they wanted to know, "Where do we go from here?"

Useful Baskets is an answer to that question, for it is more like a recipe book than the first. "How do I make a souffle or a delicious beef stew? How do I make a sturdy laundry basket or shopping basket, and what other useful objects can I turn my hand to?" The answers are in this book.

There is a sudden upsurge of interest in basketry. Gift shops, department stores, and antique shops are filled with baskets from all over the world — all ages, sizes, and types. We should approach these with due respect. Certainly their prices sometimes demand that immediately. Here is one of man's most ancient crafts — some think the oldest of all. And interestingly enough, the cheapest little basket, including those made out of plastic or coated paper, has been crafted entirely by the hand of man. Basket making has never been taken over by machines, a unique feature in our civilization.

Is this perhaps the predominant reason that basket making is so fascinating for us? Carl Jung says that the human species has a collective memory. Can it be that our interest in baskets and the relative ease with which we as beginners can make a basket is because of this ancient memory? Start off with a gentle push from Mara and there is no telling how far you will go.

I can say with confidence that you are in good hands with Mara Cary. We have a shop on Nantucket in which we sell Mara's baskets. At least we are supposed to. But so many of them find their way into my house that there is always a great shortage of them in the shop. For me they are not only very useful objects, holding plants, wool, magazines, and firewood (one I am particularly fond of goes with me to the vegetable garden to carry weeds and produce, and hangs from a rafter in the kitchen in the wintertime, promising brighter and better things to come). They are also objects of art, pieces of sculpture, as the photographs in this book show. They have the same appeal for me as a small seventeenth-century pottery Japanese tea caddy that I own. I am intimately aware of the hands that made all of these fine objects.

I not only love Mara's baskets, I love her two books and heartily recommend them to you. You can and will make many baskets using them as a guide. And in these two excellent how-to-do-it books, you will be captured by Mara's rare spirit. They do what the best of good books and good teachers do, the most important thing of all. They inspire.

ANDREW F. OATES
Nantucket 1976

Useful Baskets

I A Love for Baskets

Baskets, and the making of them, are popular today. There are lots of reasons for this. We live in a fast-paced, sophisticated world that sometimes seems to have no room for the subtleties and nuances of human beings. Baskets, by their very nature, offer a comfort, a bit of balance. They are always made by hand — no machine can do it — and they are made of "natural" stuff. They are artifacts that testify to a cooperation between man and earth.

Baskets are made essentially the same way as they always have been since man's earliest history, so they also offer a balance for our sense of time. Like any handcraft, baskets measure out a span of time, and that span of time stays locked in their forms. We can sense a kinship with native American women, with medieval Englishmen, with cave people.

Basketry needs no special equipment. A modest investment of money and time will yield results, and the results are useful.

I think that's my biggest "kick" with baskets. I am not only making things, I am making things work. I am something of an engineer. While I am making something that helps me, I can please my aesthetic senses as well. Today I can enjoy plunking a fresh-baked loaf of bread into a honeysuckle basket I made years ago in Ohio beside a railroad track.

Baskets are made of two elements: the *stakes* and the *weavers*. These are like the warp and the weft on a loom, except that the warp, or the stakes, is not held rigid by a frame. Stakes have their own strength and form, and they are the frame that is held together and filled in by the weavers. Then at the top edge the stakes work together to lock the whole basket together.

There are many ways to begin, weave, and end a basket. I present here three or four baskets made on each of several beginnings. I've filled in with a variety of weaves and topped off with a bunch of borders. You may want to copy some of my designs directly. More likely you will want to make selections — a small laundry basket for fruit, a large planter for your laundry. Or perhaps you'll make a scrap basket of yarn or a lettuce washer of honeysuckle. Whatever you do, you'll find here a festival of designs, textures, techniques, and fancies. The baskets in this book range from very easy to fairly difficult. In general, the difficulty in making a basket is directly related to size; the larger they are, the harder they are to manage. If a certain basket seems too difficult for you, make a smaller version to begin with and then work your way up. You can learn a lot that way. And you'll most likely be able to use your practice baskets, too.

It is a special joy for me to share these things with you. Basketry ranks very high with me. Right on top, along with loving and being and growing and giving. When they announce the end of the world, look for me out in the honeysuckle patch or stirring fragrant brambles in their broth. I'll be finishing a basket for Saint Peter.

If you could "hear" a basket, I think it would make a steady sound: a slow and soothing mantra, a sound of Mother in her slippers putting things in order after the children have gone to sleep.

II Materials

There are two kinds of basketry materials, those you can buy, find around the house, or recycle from something else, and those you go out into nature and harvest. The latter I shall refer to as *hedgerow materials*. I have put them together as the second half of this chapter.

Of the materials that can be purchased, the most important is *reed*. The baskets in this book are made mostly from this material. Reed is definitely the best stuff to get a start with because it is kind and mostly dependable. Occasionally you may come across some that is definitely of inferior quality. It will be pithy, stringy, and very brittle. I think you should feel free to refuse it. Send it back or do not buy it. Most of the reed available is pretty good.

Reed is also known as *rattan, kindergarten reed, center cane,* and *pulp cane.* It is a jungle vine that grows very long, climbing up on the other jungle growth by means of long thorns. When it is harvested, the bark is stripped off. Then the reed is sent to a factory to be sorted and cleaned. Various processes make it available to us as round reed, flat reed, and chair caning cane, which is strips of the inner bark.

It seems that over the years, nothing's quite as sure as change. So if you take basketry seriously enough to consult more than one book, you may very well run into great discrepancies on the sizing. What used to be size #4 is now #3, and #15 is now #6. So in order to clarify and alleviate this confusion as much as possible, I will use both the current size number and the actual measurement.

Wide flat oval reed and #4
round reed.

Sizes as of 1976:

#1   1.5 m.m.
#2   1.75 m.m.
#3   2.25 m.m.
#4   2.75 m.m.
#5   3.5 m.m.
#6   4.5 m.m.
#7   5.25 m.m.
#8   5.75 m.m.
#10   7.5 m.m.
#12   3/8 inch
1/2" round
Narrow flat oval 1/4"
Wide flat oval 3/8"
Flat 1/4"
Flat 3/8"
Flat 1/2"
Half-round #6

My philosophy on the subject of soaking reed (and this goes for any material that requires soaking) is this: respect the life. Essentially what we are doing with reed, and indeed all natural basketry materials, is borrowing the time between its growth and its ultimate deterioration. Once it is cut from its roots, it is bound to die, so we step in and ask it to help us on its way out. Naturally, the better the care we give it, the more life it will have for the work we ask of it. When it comes to soaking, I do as little as possible but as much as necessary.

Approximate soaking times:

#1 and #2	pass through the water
#3	5 minutes
#4	10 minutes
#5	15 minutes
#6	20 minutes

Once soaked, keep the reed between layers of damp toweling. Do not keep it wet overnight. Allow it to dry, and then resoak it the next day.

The way I do it is to soak a few weavers at a time. Then as I weave I get to take a break and stand up to pull and coil and soak some more. Say there are six weavers in the water. When I get down to one, I throw in six more, use the last one,

Reed soaking.

This is a copy of a reticule made with #2 reed. The original was lined with green silk and highlighted with green glass beads.

A sewing basket made by Ginny Cianciolo.

and by that time the new ones are ready. I generally use warm water because it feels pleasant.

Raffia is another familiar craft product. It is, however, a little more difficult to work with than reed. But get acquainted with it; it has a lot of uses. Raffia is a layer split from large palm leaves and then split into strips. It can be used as a weaver as is, or braided, twisted, or finger-woven and then used as a weaver. Usually raffia does not require soaking, but soaking won't hurt it. The only time I soak it is to flatten it out, as it tends to curl upon itself. Raffia can be dyed effectively.

Fiber rush and *Fiber splint* are made of paper and glue to be used as substitutes for rush and splints in chair seating. Both are fun to use in baskets. Neither should be gotten wet as both tend to come apart.

Hong Kong Grass is a pretty, ropelike twisted sea grass. It smells good for a long time. It is the most natural-looking of all commercial basket materials. A basket made entirely of Hong Kong Grass may be too heavy, but it makes an excellent weaver on reed stakes. Hong Kong Grass need not be soaked.

This was an experiment in newspaper. Half the basket was painted with gesso. Gesso gives the newspaper a hard, paintable surface.

If you have trouble with the ends untwisting, dip them in glue or bind them with thread or fine wire.

Wire includes silver, gold, copper, telephone wire, plastic, etc.
Yarns and *twines* means everything from goat wool to baling twine.
Strips of fabrics are used much as one makes a braided rug.
Sash cord means clothesline and jump rope.
Newspaper is folded into strips.

SOURCES OF REED AND OTHER BASKET MATERIALS

Ace Rattan Products, 60–19 54th Place, Maspeth, New York 11378

Bamboo and Rattan Works, 901 Jefferson St., Hoboken, New Jersey 07030

Cane and Basket Supply Co., 1283 South Cochran Ave., Los Angeles, California 90019

Coulter Studios, 118 East 59th St., New York, New York 10022

Creative Handweavers, P.O. Box 26480, Los Angeles, California 90026 (Palm Strips)

8

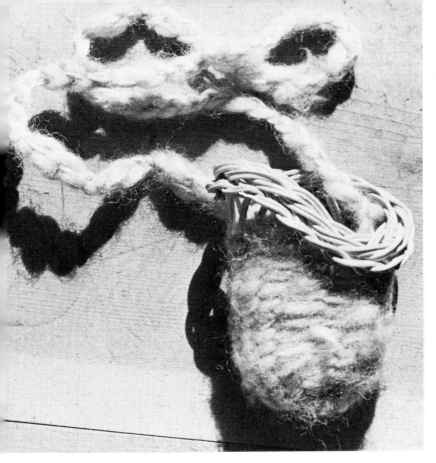

A mohair and reed watch pocket.

Earth Guild Incorporated, 149 Putnam Ave., Cambridge, Massachusetts 02139

H. H. Perkins Co., 10 South Bradley Road, Woodbridge, Connecticut 06525

Natural Craft, 2199 Bancroft Way, Berkeley, California 94704

New Hampshire Cane and Reed Co., 65 Turnpike St., Suncook, New Hampshire 03275

Peerless Rattan and Reed Co., 97 Washington St., New York, New York 10016

The Clay People, 3345 N. Halstead, Chicago, Illinois, 60657 (Beads)

Whitaker Reed Co., 90 May St., Box 172, Worcester, Massachusetts 01602

HEDGEROW MATERIALS

I use the term "hedgerow" for two reasons. The first is a reason of the heart. I have always loved the word, which I first heard as the name of a rather special theater in Virginia that nurtured some special actors and actresses who in turn

Dyed #4 round reed and brambles.

nurtured my young theater experiences. I also like the word hedgerow because it brings to mind the actual process of being out there by a hedge, whereas "natural" these days often conjures up images of bright green shampoo in a plastic bottle or honey-coated oats with no preservatives added. Anyway, reed and raffia are also natural. This section is about that which you can nurture or gather out there among the hedges, mountains and trees, dells and beaches.

Do use care in gathering. I know you will, for anyone who is on a collecting mission is aware of the needs of the earth. But I could not let my conscience rest if I encouraged someone to go a-gathering without warning him not to leave as much as a gum wrapper where it did not belong, to say nothing of cigarette filters or (shudder) bottles or cans.

And keep in mind the old adage about wildflowers: "For every one you pick, leave ten behind." If you go out in unfamiliar areas, find out what plants are legally protected or should be. Beach grass on Nantucket is too busy holding sand in place for me to borrow any.

Basketry materials are not limited to plants, however. There is no reason why other things cannot be gathered from the hedgerow. Seashells, animal teeth, wings of insects, bones; wool from sheep, goats, llama or Samoyed dogs; horses' tail hair and sinew thread. And, of course, feathers and porcupine quills have always been used and still can be if they are available.

The following is a list I gathered more from research at my desk than from the wild. It is not meant to be exhaustive, or indeed exhausting, to the reader. I found the research stimulating and can't wait to finish this writing so I can go out exploring some more in the field. I offer my findings in hopes that you may find something useful.

Fig. 1 Boiling brambles.

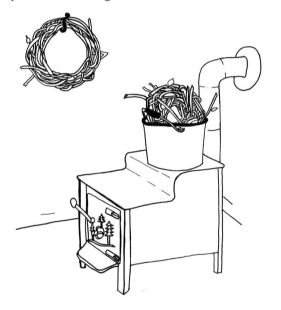

Vines

I have a basic honeysuckle recipe that I use for all vines. I know it works, that's why I use it. It may not be necessary to boil all vines, and maybe not for four hours, but it can't hurt and it does make them easier to handle. I do encourage experimentation, however.

Basic Vine Recipe

Gather the vines any time (though fall and winter probably are better). Clean off the leaves and thorns, unless you want them to influence the color. Blackberry leaves, for example, give a ruddy hue to the vines. Boil or steam for four hours. Let cool. Rinse. Use. Or, dry to store and resoak for a few minutes to use.

In the following list I have added any comments I've heard, found, or thought of that seem useful, even if they disagree with the above recipe. You will see that there are other possibilities.

Blackberry brambles may be peeled, in which case they look rather like commercial reed, or they can be used with their bark. If a very tight weave is necessary, they should be peeled, since the bark swells a little when wet and then of course dries smaller after you've woven with it. Wear gloves and do a good job of cleaning off the thorns.

A bramble basket made by Shelby Stancioff.

12

Grapevine has its very own distinctive shape and curlicues. I usually peel it down to the last dark inner bark, but I leave that on for the color. The bark that gets peeled off can be used in coil baskets. Sometimes when I make baskets with grapevine handles, I've oiled the vine with vegetable oil, which brings out its color. I put the oil on with a paintbrush, let it stand overnight, then wash the basket in soapy water to get off any excess. (Oil brings out the color of reed, too.)

Honeysuckle vine is one of my oldest favorites. I know a secret place where it grows from all sides out into a little grassy clearing. I call that place "honeysuckle heaven." It's so easy to gather there and there's so much of it. There are deer there, and I have the owner's permission to gather. My son, Donick, who's always finding money, once found three dollars there.

Honeysuckle is so kind to the person working with it. It's pretty and it's strong. It peels very easily. When it's wet you can just clean the bark off with a cloth.

Ivy, Boston and English, looks good with or without bark. My friend Shelby, and I once climbed over a fence into somebody's backyard to haul off some from a pile of English ivy that had just been thinned out. I felt like Huck Finn.

Wild Strawberries can make teeny-tiny baskets. I only boil them half an hour.

Roses, if they are the viny kind, can be tamed just like blackberry vines. Wear gloves. Clean off the thorns before you boil the vines. They can be split if they are too thick.

Wisteria bark can only be removed with a knife, but it can be woven in, too.

Bark

Bark must be taken from living trees, but doing so destroys the tree. However, if I lived near a woods I'd be out there thinning out the saplings. The idea here is to pick branches with the least amount of twigs, which get in the way. Cut the branches into lengths you can handle (3 to 4 feet) and "carve" off the bark. Put one end on the ground, the other in one hand. Brace the ground end against your foot and whittle downward with one long stroke to lift off each strip of bark. If you are debarking a sapling, you can leave it in the ground until you've stripped it.

These are the best trees to look for:

Basswood
Black Walnut (inner bark)
Cedar (I got some from some new fenceposts)
Elm (inner bark)
Hazel
Indian Hemp
Oregon Maple (white inner bark)
Paper Birch (would be stripped round and round, I expect)
Redbud
Red Mulberry

Grasses, Leaves, and Stems

In general, grasses, leaves, and stems must be cured so that they have done all their shrinking before you begin weaving.

Cut them with scissors. Cut them green and dry them in the sun to get a white color. Cut them green and dry them in the shade for a green color. Cut them brown for a brown color.

To dry grasses, hang them upside-down in bundles in an airy space. Beware of hot, dry attics and mildewy basements. Grasses should dry slowly. After about a week, use them or wrap them in paper for storing. Soak them until they are pliable enough to use. Some grasses such as the flat-leaved kind are ready in ten to fifteen minutes. The round-stemmed kind may take two or three hours.

Bamboo. I've seen it growing in gardens so I'll include it. Young canes are used, 1 to 3 inches in diameter. Cut and split them into quarters or eighths or more. Scrape out the pithy center. They can then be stored indefinitely. Bamboo is tough and hard to weave. Soak it for as long as you can — a week to ten days. Keep it very wet. It makes strong baskets.

Bromegrass. Split the stems.

Broomcorn.

Bullrush (Tule). Strips of stem and strips of root are also usable.

Cattail leaves. Strip off the center vein. Dry the leaves in shallow piles, turning them occasionally. They will shrink, so gather more than you think you will need. Soak them *only* five to ten minutes.

Iris leaves.

Lake sedge grows ten feet tall with flowers that look like dark brown tufted feathers. They are, it is said, usually just beyond wading distance in places much frequented by eels. Hip boots might help here. Cut the sedge when the flowers come into bloom, about the beginning of July. Dry the stalks, out of direct sunlight, and turn them several times. Tie them up in bundles and stand them on their butt ends to store.

Preparation: In damp weather dip a bundle in water and wrap it in an old blanket or sack to mellow for twenty-four hours. In dry weather soak the sedge ten to fifteen minutes, then wrap it to mellow.

Work in a moist environment. Sedge gets dry and brittle quickly. Oversoaked, it turns pulpy. It feels like velvet ribbon when it is just right.

Sedge can be braided or finger-woven into strips to weave or sew together. It can also be twisted.

Long moss hangs on Southern swamp trees.

Martynia (Devil's-horn).

Milkweed stem.

Pine needles. Soak a few at a time for a few minutes.

Rush or wire grass.

Seneca grass (Holy grass or Vanilla grass).

Stinging nettle. I've heard that nettle fiber can be made into fine, fine fabric, good for sheets.

Straw. Use wheat, rye, or rice.

Sweet grass (Vernal).

Wormwood. Use the stems.

Shoots and Branches

I would recommend using the basic vine recipe on any of these. Or try one of the willow recipes below.

Bittersweet.

California lilac.

Calycanthus or *Strawberry shrub.* Use the wood and bark from young shoots.

Cottonwood.

Greenbrier.

Hazel.

Hazelnut.

Mulberry.

Poplar.

Privet.

Rabbit brush, Rabbit bush. I don't know if they are the same thing. They are more flexible in summer. The bark can be removed after soaking. The sapwood can be cut into strips.

Redbud twigs. Gather them in winter. Split them in half to dry in the sun. Scrape the twigs down to equal thickness if you want to. Take only a small number from each tree.

Red osier dogwood.

Serviceberry.

Smilax.

Snowberry.

Sumac.

Syringa.

White birch.

Willow. There are many kinds: American green willow, almond leafed willow, golden willow, weeping willow, purple willow, and pussy willow.

When I was weaving baskets in the window of Barclays Bank in Boston, a woman passed by, stopped, and then came in. She had such a thick Welsh accent I was immediately charmed. She told me that she and her grandfather used to go down by "the river" and "do that." She said, "We used to use the Sally rods." The Latin generic name for willow is *Salix.*

Harvest the shoots of one year's growth for baskets. Cut them close to the main stem, leaving a little stump that will then sprout many new shoots for the next year.

I have found several systems for "curing" the harvested willow, which is called a "rod."

If you want peeled "white" rods, cut the shoots in the spring when the leaves are budding. Peel them within a day or two, using a small knife, your fingers, and a little time and patience. The rods may be dyed at this time or dried and stored. You can dye the rods just before use as well. When you want to use them, soak them for three days, and then wrap them in a damp cloth until you use them.

Other methods of preparing white rods: Harvest them in the early spring when the sap is just rising; the bark will loosen a little so you can scrape a little of it off with a thumbnail.

To peel off the rest of the bark:

16

a) Lay the shoots on wet soil with some old willow peelings and let them ferment in the heat for several weeks. When the bark loosens, strip it from the rods, wash the rods clean and dry them in the sun to keep them from molding.
b) Stand up bundles of rods in buckets of water until the first leaves appear. Then peel, wash, and dry.
c) Steam the rods for one to four hours, peel them, and wash and dry them.

Before using, soak the willow rods in warm water for an hour and then wrap them in a damp cloth to soften and mellow.

For tan or "buffed" rods, cut the shoots in fall after the leaves have gone, or through the winter before the sap rises in the spring. Boil four to six hours. The boiling is called "buffing." When cool, peel the bark off and dry the rods in the sun and air. To use the rods, soak them for an hour in warm water, then wrap them in a damp cloth.

Harvest brown willow rods in the late autumn to early spring (before the sap rises). Dry the rods in the wind and sun. Soak them in warm water for three or four days and then wrap them in a wet cloth for one day more before using.

Willow can be split to make finer, more pliable weavers. The splits are called skeins.

Ornaments and Decorations

Bayberries.
Beads. Use beads from old costume jewelry or from bead companies. You can use wood, clay, or gemstone.
Cockleburrs or *Burdock.*
Cork.
Cornhusks.
Drawer pulls for feet or handles.
Dried flowers.
Leather strips. My cousin Judy gave me some from a nearby saddle factory.
Milkweed pods. Or use any pretty seed pod.
Paper strips. Explore local printers' scrap baskets.
Teasel.
TV tape or *old film.*
Seaweed.
Seashells.
Warp ends from a friendly weaver.

III Finishes, Colors, and Dyes

There are times when colors add new dimensions of fun and beauty to baskets. I always try to start out a new class of students with some variety of colors. Their first baskets will then have the distinction of their own choice of colors right away, and colors help beginners to tell things apart and thus make the process of learning easier. Learning, in my opinion, should always be made as easy as possible. Baskets that are to be used outdoors will benefit from a protective coat of something. Or you might want to color-key a basket to the decorating scheme of a room.

FINISHES

Baskets can be finished and colored in a number of ways. A wax, stain, paint, or preservative can be applied after the basket is woven. The material can be dyed before the basket is woven, or the finished basket can be dyed.

First, let's consider applied finishes. These would include just about anything that is appropriate to finish wood.

1. Turpentine and varnish, half and half.
2. Linseed oil, three parts, and turpentine, one part.
3. Stain, one part; turpentine, two parts; and linseed oil, one part.

4. Any commercial stain-wax product, thinned with turpentine.
5. Vegetable oil, painted on, left overnight, and the excess washed off with soapy water, for baskets to be used with food.
6. Paints, thinned out a little with whatever thinner is appropriate for the type of paint. Thinning makes the paint easier to apply evenly. Paints such as oils and acrylics can also be rubbed on with a cloth.
7. Dying, as I have said, can be done before or after the basket is woven. Dying the material first allows for decorative weaving. Dyed baskets can also then be finished as above.

Before dying the reed, wash it first in soap and water, then rinse it well to remove any traces of sulfur that will affect the color. Before dying raffia, soak it in cold water for an hour. This will help to congeal the natural resins that help to keep it from shredding.

There are two basic types of dying: store-bought and vegetable or "natural" dyes. When using store-bought dyes, follow the directions for hand-dying. These colors will fade some, with the possible exception of batik dyes. Keep in mind that colors look darker when wet. I sometimes like to dye reed unevenly on purpose as I did in my tie-dyed scrap basket.

NATURAL DYES

When it comes to vegetable dyes, I'm afraid the colors will not be as spectacular as they can be when these vegetable dyes are used on wool. With almost no exceptions, basket materials are from vegetable sources, and for some reason vegetable dyes do not have such dramatic changes on vegetable fibers as they do on animal fibers. Baskets, however, are most often wanted in subtle hues, so here is my recipe:

Use an enamel or stainless steel pot. Aluminum and iron affect the color. Do *not* use cooking pots, as some of the dyes are poisonous. Be sure to store the chemicals out of the reach of children. If you will be doing a lot of dying, it is worth purchasing an enamel pail. Use a wooden spoon or a clean stick to stir with and to lift the material out of the mordant or dye bath.

If your water is hard water, add a little water softener, or use rainwater.

The material to be dyed must first be "mordanted." This is a process that prepares the material to take as much color as possible. Before mordanting reed, wash it in soapy water and rinse it well. Raffia should be soaked in cold water for an hour.

Any cotton mordant recipe may be used. Here is the recipe I use. This recipe takes four days to do, but my experience has been that the extra color gained is worth the patience.

For one pound of dry material to be dyed, you will need:

— eight ounces of alum (potassium aluminum sulfate). This must be ordered from a chemical supplier, since the alum the drugstore sells is not the right kind for dying. See the source list at the end of this chapter.

— two ounces of washing soda, which can be purchased at the supermarket.

— one ounce of tannic acid, which drugstores and chemical suppliers carry.

Directions:

1. Dissolve 4 ounces of alum and 1 ounce of washing soda in 4½ gallons of cold water; wet the material; put it in the bath; heat slowly and simmer for one hour; remove from heat and let it sit overnight.
2. On the second day remove the material from the bath and rinse it in clear soft water; put it into a new bath of 1 ounce of tannic acid and 4½ gallons of soft water; heat the bath and let it simmer for one hour; remove from heat, and let it sit again overnight.
3. On the third day, rinse the material again and put it into a new bath of 4 ounces of alum, 1 ounce of washing soda, and 4 gallons of water. Simmer one hour, cool, and leave overnight.
4. On the fourth day, rinse the material once more. Now it can be dyed, or it may be dried and dyed later.

There are many natural dye sources. The ones I've used successfully include blackberry and honeysuckle vines and leaves, goldenrod blossoms, marigold blossoms, zinnia blossoms, onion skins, blackberries, elderberries, pokeberries, sumac berries, vibernum berries, apple twigs and leaves, sassafras root, dandelion stems and roots, black walnut hulls (these do not need a mordant), wild grapes, Welch's grape juice, pine needles, and peanut shells.

It takes about a pound of source material to dye a pound of reed. The more you use the stronger the color.

To make a dye bath, chop or crush the source material and soak it overnight; bring it to a boil and simmer it for an hour; strain it through a colander or cheesecloth, and that's your dye bath.

To dye the mordanted basket material, immerse it in the dye bath; bring it to a boil; simmer one to two hours; remove from dye bath and rinse.

SOURCES OF DYE CHEMICALS AND NATURAL DYES

Cushings Perfection Dyes, W. Cushing and Co., Dover-Foxcroft, Maine 04426

Kem Chemical Co., 545 S. Fulton St., Mount Vernon, New York 10550

Straw Into Gold, 5500 College Ave., Oakland, California 94618

Wide World of Herbs Ltd., 11 Catherine St. East, Montreal, 129P. Quebec, Canada

IV Words and Tools

TOOLS

You only need your hands and your teeth, but you may find some of these things helpful:

APRON —— Heavy enough to keep you dry, maybe with pockets.

AWL —— Or steel knitting needle or bodkin.

A BASIN OR SINK, TUB OR PAIL —— To soak in.

CLIP-TYPE CLOTHESPINS.

ROUND-NOSED PLIERS —— Or needle-nosed pliers.

RULER —— Or footrule, measuring tape, or yardstick.

SCISSORS —— Or sidecutters, clippers.

SPONGE.

WORDS

Mark this page with a piece of reed or grass — you may want to refer to it often if you haven't made baskets before.

BASE —— The bottom of the basket, which is almost invariably woven first.

BORDER —— The top or opening edge of the basket, which is almost invariably woven last.

BREAKING DOWN —— Dividing up a group of stakes into smaller groups or single stakes.

BUTTON —— You will see this term used in other books to refer to the center.

BYE STAKE OR BI-STAKE —— A stake inserted to make an odd number of stakes to facilitate certain weaving patterns.

CENTER —— This is the term I use to mean the very first couple of rounds that bind the stakes together.

CHANGE —— In some situations it is necessary to correct a weave once each round so that it can continue its pattern. This point of correction is called a "change," which is short for "change-of-stroke."

COIL —— Although coiling is a whole type of basket weaving in itself, a coil in this context refers to one round of *three rod wale* or some other wale that is finished by inserting the ends into the spot of their own beginning and is used to define a pattern or strengthen or help shape a basket.

CROWNING —— The making of a slightly concave bottom to a basket for the purpose of letting the basket stand up straight.

JOIN —— Another word for splice.

NEEDLES AND THREADS —— On bases where the center is made by making a slit in some of the stakes, the bases are called "needles;" the bases that are threaded through are called "threads."

SLYPE —— I just love this word. It rhymes with "ripe." It means a long diagonal cutoff to a stake to facilitate insertion into weaving or to a handle core for the same reason.

SPLICE —— As a verb, this means what you do when you run out of weaver. The noun means that which was done.

SPOKES —— What other folks call "stakes."

STAKES —— The spokes, ribs, staves, warp, or strong upright members of the basket into which the weaver is woven.

STROKE —— One motion of the weaver, or that unit of activity which is repeated over and over to accomplish the weaving.

UPSETT —— The term "to upsett" means to set up the stakes; the noun is that point at which the stakes are bent upward.

WEAVER —— The long flexible pieces that bind together and fill in between the stakes.

Basket of flat reed, jute, and #5
round reed.

GETTING TO WORK

Take a little time to assemble your tools and materials. Find a way to hang up the roll of reeds or somehow secure them so that you can take out one at a time (after the first few, with one hand).

It is even helpful ahead of time to find a place to put everything away. The obvious solution is, of course, to weave a big basket to hold it all. But a closet or corner or garage or a box under the bed will do.

The weaving itself may be thought of as "laying in" the weaver between the stakes. Each stroke that is laid in fixes its shape in the basket so one weaves the shape that the basket will be. Consider also the distance between stakes. For symmetry, space them evenly apart. To flare out the sides, push the stakes farther apart. To arrive at an assymetrical shape, add extra stakes for more space.

To make bottoms that stand well, if that's what you want:

a) Make a "crowned" or slightly concave bottom.
b) Add wooden beads or some other type of feet.
c) Work very flat on a table and then, for a few rounds before the upsett, use a heavier weave such as *three rod wale* with a heavier-size reed.

My summer studio.

V Weaves

Fig. 2 *In-and-out* weave.

Fig. 3 You control the weaver to put the stakes in place.

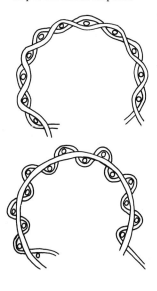

Fig. 4 Spiral ridge formed by "change of stroke."

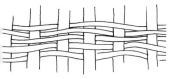

"Randing, waling,
slewing and slypes;
no matter what the start,
the finish is always heart-shaped."

— Anonymous

In-and-out weave is also known as *randing, simple* weave, and *under-and-over* weave (Fig. 2). This is certainly the simplest weave to comprehend; the weaver goes in and out and in and out. But it is not necessarily the best weave for one's first few baskets, because it's not a good weave to shape with. The rule "Do not let the weaver master the stakes" applies here. Use a weaver that's smaller than the stakes. When working *in-and-out* weave, use your thumb and first finger to "place" or "wrap" the weaver in and out between the stakes (Fig. 3).

If worked on an even number of stakes, the weave has to be corrected or "changed" at the beginning of each round. This is very easily accomplished by going over or under two stakes at the start of the second round. This will be seen to form a ridge, which spirals up the side of the basket (Fig. 4). The change becomes almost automatic as the weaving is worked. There are several ways to avoid a change. One can simply arrange to weave two stakes together as one, cut one off, or add a bye stake to arrive at an uneven number of stakes. Or one can do *chasing* weave (see next page).

Decorative possibilities with *in-and-out* weave include:

— horizontal stripes of color or texture (other materials)
— colored stakes and natural weaver and vice versa

Chasing is really a variation of *in-and-out* done with two weavers, one round with one, the next one with the other, on an odd or even number of stakes (Fig. 5).

Interesting decorative textures can be done with two different weavers, say one weaver of #2 reed and one of Hong Kong Grass, or four-as-one of #2 reed, or flat reed (Fig. 6).

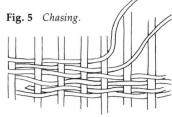

Fig. 5 *Chasing.*

Slewing is another variation of *in-and-out* weave, done with two or more weavers used together as one. It is an example of the fine vocabulary of technical terms that the rich English basket-weaving tradition and history offer us. *Slewing* comes from willow work and is often seen in large willow baskets. It is useful if you want to hurry up and get the sides woven. A little care is needed to keep the weavers from twisting (Fig. 7).

Fig. 6 *Chasing variation.*

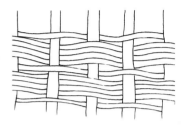

French randing also is a direct descendant of willow basketry and is often seen in bicycle baskets. It is done to make good use of relatively shorter willow rods, which are thicker at the butt end than at the tip. It is applicable to any shortish shoots you might use, such as bush honeysuckle, hazel, and, of course, willow. I've always meant to try it on a scrap basket with several colors of reed (Fig. 8).

Fig. 7 *Slewing.*

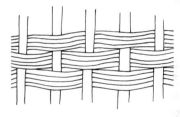

Japanese weave, also known as *rib randing*, is illustrated in Figures 9 and 10. This weave can be done with any number of weavers. The number of stakes should not be evenly divisible by three. The weave is *under-one-over-two*. (It can also be done *over-one-under-two*.)

Fig. 8 *French randing.*

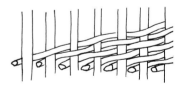

Colonial weave is the weave that is known as "basket weave" to a textile weaver. It is done with one weaver *over-*

Fig. 9 *Japanese* weave.

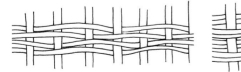

Fig. 10 *Japanese* weave.

Fig. 11 *Colonial* weave or *Basket* weave.

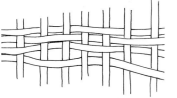

Fig. 12 *Packing*.

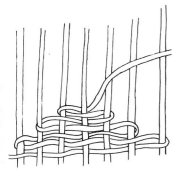

two-under-two on any number of stakes not evenly divisible by four (Fig. 11).

a) If the number of stakes is divisible by four with a remainder of two (30-34-38), the weave must be changed at the beginning of each round by going behind one.
b) Stakes divisible by four plus three (31-35-39) make a coil slanting up to the right.
c) Stakes divisible by four plus one (29-33-37) make a coil slanting up to the left.

Packing is the name of *in-and-out* woven back and forth to fill in a space or fill out a shape (Fig. 12).

Under-one-over-four is one of many possibilities you can invent (Fig. 13).

Fig. 13 *Under-one-over-four.*

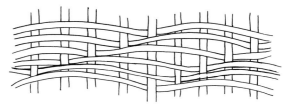

Fig. 14 *Wraparound* weave.

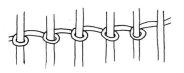

Wraparound probably has a proper name, but I do not know it. It can only be done with flexible weavers such as yarns or twines (Fig. 14).

Brick weave is *wraparound* done inside-out with cane or flat reed (Fig. 15).

Fig. 15 *Brick* weave.

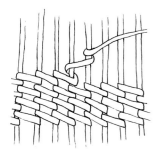

Bellefonte weave must have been invented for strong baskets where it was necessary to have lots of stakes. Done on a num-

Fig. 16 *Bellefonte* weave.

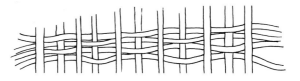

ber of stakes divisible by four with a remainder of two (18, 22, 26), it is *over-one-under-three*. It must be done in conjunction with some other weave as every other stake gets "left out" as it were (Fig. 16).

Fig. 17 *Twining ("S" twist).*

Twining, also known as *pairing,* is one of my old standbys. It's a good weave for controlling shape, surpassed only in my opinion by *three rod wale. Twining* is very pleasant to do as of course most all of this is. *Twining* is done with two weavers on any number of stakes. It can go in either direction and twist in an "S" twist or a "Z" twist (Figs. 17, 18, 19).

Fig. 18 *Twining.*

Designs done in *twining:*

a) One plain and one colored, weaver on an odd number of stakes make a spiral.
b) One plain and one colored weaver on an even number of stakes make vertical stripes.

Fig. 19 *Twining ("Z" twist).*

A checkered effect can be gotten by changing the two weavers at even intervals (say, every five rows, or whatever measures about right).

Fig. 20 Double twist.

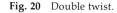

Double twist is *twining* with an extra twist between each stake. It is especially effective with two different weavers (Fig. 20).

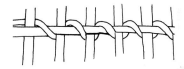

Arrow, also known as *chain pairing,* is a row of *twining* in an "S" twist on top of a row of "Z" twist or vice versa (Fig. 21).

Fig. 21 *Arrow weave.*

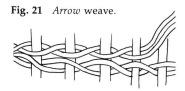

Fitching is another fancy British term for twining rows with lots of space between them. The stakes can be rearranged in different ways between rows of *fitching.* When the row is "fitched," the ends are tucked in beside their beginnings for the sake of holding them there as well as looking good (Fig. 22).

Fig. 22 *Fitching.*

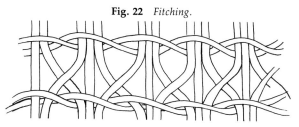

Waling, pronounced "wailing," is usually *three rod wale*, but it can be *four rod wale, five rod wale,* etc. Once set up, the actual weaving is just as simple as *twining.* It is very helpful to use whenever you are having trouble getting the shape you want, for instance, at the upsett or just before the border. It really makes sure the stakes are as evenly spaced as possible. It can be used to frame a pattern, or it can be the weave (Figs. 23, 24). *Three rod wale* is *over-two-under-one. Four rod wale* is *over-three-under-one* or *over-two-under-two. Five rod wale* is *over-four-under-one* or *over-three-under-two.*

Fig. 23 *Three rod wale.*

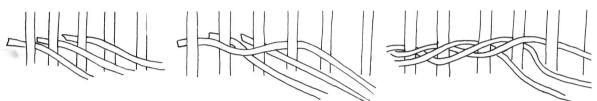

Fig. 24 *Four rod wale.*

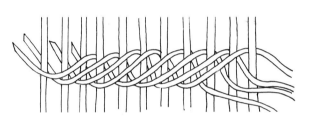

Decorative possibilities for *three rod wale* include:

a) Three different colors of weavers on a number of stakes divisible by three (four for *four rod wale*) yields three colors of vertical stripes.
b) One color and two natural weavers on stakes divisible by three plus one yields a spiral inside and a variegated effect outside.
c) One color and two natural weavers on stakes divisible by three plus two gives a spiral outside and a variegated inside.

X weave is done with one weaver of flat reed and two weavers of #2 round reed (Fig. 25).

Fig. 25 *X weave.*

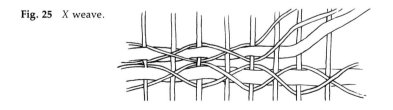

VI Handles

Suit the basket to the need and the handle to the basket. Thou canst not then be false to any purpose.

Here are a few techniques for making handles.

The simplest would be to tie something across the top. Figure 26 shows the simplest reed handle.

The knot handle is a "quick and easy" handle. It's not very strong, but it is useful for trinkets and containers for dry flowers, etc. It is made by threading two pairs of stakes (or triplets) down through the border (or from the outside in behind some rows of weaving and back out). The bottom ends are then made into this knot (Fig. 27) or some approximation thereof. The top pairs are then twisted or braided or whatever (they could be filled with a bright yarn woven in) and their ends threaded through and made into a knot on the other side. The remaining ends can then be tucked in between rows of weaving and cut off.

The "roped" handle wears well and looks great. For some reason I always like it to look a little stronger than it needs to be and have run into the problem of having my handle master my basket. Two solutions are to carve down the handle core so it is not so domineering and to notch it out so you can control the shape (Fig. 28).

If you are using hedgerow material for the core of the handle and it does not bend easily into the desired shape, heat it up by boiling or steaming, bend it slowly into shape, and tie it off (a little too tight is best). Let it dry out completely. If you are doing two handles the same size, bend them together.

Fig. 26 Simplest reed handle.

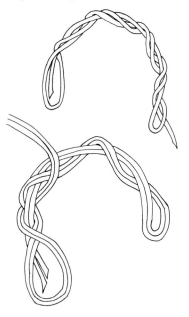

Fig. 27 Knot handle.

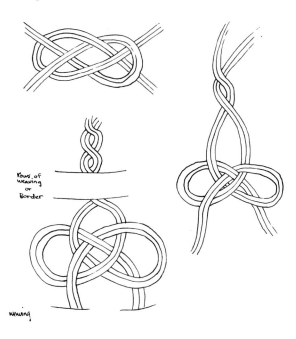

Rows of
weaving
or
Border

weaving

Fig. 28 Roped handle.

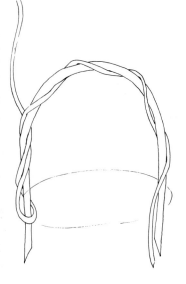

Fig. 29a Warp handle.

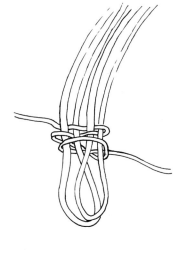

Fig. 29b Wrapped handle.

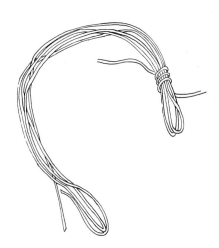

Carryall

Carved handle of #8 round reed.

Handle inserted into sides of basket.

Beginning the wrapping.

Partially wrapped handle.

A Hong Kong Grass warp filled in with jute.

Another way of making a secure "strap" is to thread a sort of warp for yourself and then fill it in, or wrap around it (Figs. 29A, 29B).

The photo below shows my own invention. It is made like Figure 29B but made *off* the basket. The handle then buttons on over the drawer pulls. I used #2 reed and went back and forth six times all together. This idea might be of use to potters for a teapot's handle.

Garden basket.

VII Round Baskets

EASIEST BASKET

Actually, once I had named the "easiest basket," I discovered two others that equally deserve the name. I hit on this recipe one day when I was in a "production" mood. I must have made fifteen or twenty baskets that day — all based on this idea. This is the only one I kept; in fact I kept it as a record. The others were larger and of various shapes. I probably used more stakes in some of them than in this one.

You will need:

Easiest basket.

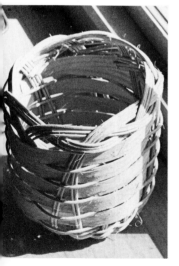

#4 reed
one or two pieces of inch-wide flat reed

Fig. 30

Cut sixteen stakes of #4 reed 25 inches long.

Soak them.

Arrange them as in Figure 30.

Soak a few #4 weavers.

Begin weaving *over-and-under* each group of four. Go around three times, then pinch the weaver and go back the other way three times around.

Add another weaver, and break down each group of four into two pairs of stakes. Do two rounds, then upsett the stakes for the sides as you weave the next three rounds.

Now, weaving over two pair, or four stakes, again do the *chasing* weave with one #4 and the inch-wide flat reed.

When you run out of flat reed, or when sides are woven about 5 inches high, do the basic border, using each group of four stakes as if it were one.

This basket could be made with more stakes by using the center in Figure 31.

Fig. 31

Tea strainer.

TEA STRAINER

On this model the handle is made by looping the weaver on the three top rows. Then the border is worked. I've also made these with handles added after the border is finished. The handles are not only to hold, they prop the strainer on the rim of the cup. These tea strainers actually work quite well. They make great gifts with a package of loose tea, which is always cheaper than tea bags.

I've also made larger baskets, which I use as colanders.

You will need:

some #2 reed

Cut eight stakes, 9½ inches long.

Do the first four rounds of the center in Figure 32. Then do *Japanese* weave, *over-two-under-one,* and upsett while your work is still small enough to fit inside a teacup. The handle can be any shape you like.

Fig. 32

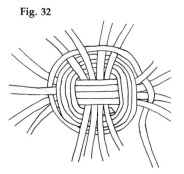

38

PENCIL BASKET

This basket could also have been called the "easiest." Of course I have made many baskets by now and easy is a relative term. If these baskets are not easy for you, make a few of them or some others. Give your hands a chance to learn how to handle and shape the material.

You will need:

#2 reed

Cut sixteen stakes of #2 reed, 16 inches long.

Soak the stakes and six or seven weavers.

Arrange the sixteen stakes as in Figure 32.

Weave *over-and-under* each group of four stakes for four rounds. Pinch the weaver and go back the other way for one round. Pinch and go back again in the opposite direction for four rounds, back the other way for one round, and then four more in the original direction.

Pencil basket.

Fig. 33 *Inside-one-and-out.*

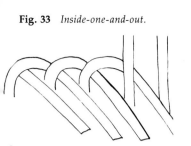

Fig. 34

Now, break down to two stakes and weave *in-and-out* for four or five rounds to upsett. Then, going back to groups of four stakes, weave again four rounds forward and one reversed. At the point of reversal each time, I interlaced the weaver but that is not necessary.

The border is done with only the two outside stakes of each group. Cut off the other two stakes flush with the top of the weaving. Using each stake that's left, weave the border (Fig. 33). Then do three rounds of the border (Fig. 34).

GRETCHEN'S BASKET

This basket is so pleasing to me. It's just perfect — one of those where the shape and technique please the eye, the feel charms the hand, and the handle is sturdy enough to hold whatever gets put in the space below. It smells good, and we can trust it to "carry on" for the next fifty or hundred years. I like the bottom weave (*Japanese* weave) so much I used it for the laundry basket on the inside so I can see it when I do the wash. Another wonderful thing about this basket is that although it is made with heavy reed, it is "simply" made and goes together smoothly. The border is really sturdy.

You will need:

#6 reed
#4 reed
#6 half-round reed
Hong Kong Grass
28 inches of #10 reed for handle

Cut and soak eight 48-inch stakes of #6 reed and fifteen 22-inch stakes of the same. Soak a couple of weavers of #4 and six #6 half-round weavers.

Using the 48-inch stakes, do the center as shown in Figure 31. It is just four rounds over and under the groups of four stakes with a #4 weaver. Then begin the *Japanese* weave (over-two-under-one) and weave a circle 4 inches wide. Now insert the fifteen shorter stakes. One of the stakes already in the circle will not have a partner. That means there are thirty-one stakes, which is appropriate for both the *Japanese* weave and the *in-and-out* weave. Continue the *Japanese* weave using the #6 half-round, and when the base measures approximately 6½ inches high, work the border as follows:

Round one: Each stake goes inside of two and out as in Figure 35. For round two, see Figure 36. For round three, go outside of the next two and back inside as in Figure 37. For round four, see Figure 34. Trim the stakes.

A roped handle, carefully shaped, completes the work.

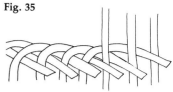

Fig. 35

Fig. 36

Fig. 37

Gretchen's basket.

SEWING BASKET

My mother asked for a sewing basket for Christmas, so this is her project. I will have made a round ruffled pincushion to attach inside the top by the time you read this, but I haven't yet. I've always had a liking for brown velvet and for Mom. So I put some velvet ribbon in her basket.

You will need:

#2 reed

For the bottom, cut seventeen stakes 28 inches long. I use seventeen so the *Japanese* weave will work.

The center begins like the one in Figure 31, but after five rounds I pinch the weaver and fold it back on itself, going five more rounds in the other direction in the same manner as shown in Figure 32.

Japanese weave is done for most of the bottom over pairs of stakes or *over-four-under-two*.

Just before the upsett, when the base measures about 5½ inches (the whole base measures 7 inches), I break down to single stakes by means of two rounds of *three rod wale* (Fig. 23). Then I go back to *Japanese* weave (over-two-under-one). About an inch up the side I weave in a round of velvet ribbon which I tie into a bow. The sides go up 2 more inches.

Fig. 38

The border is one round (Fig. 33). The second round is like Figure 38 except over four and back inside. Be careful of the ends of the stakes. Be sure that they are wet enough not to break.

The rim inside, which holds the top, is made by weaving two rounds of *twining* on those leftover stakes. Then do another border (Figs. 33, 38).

For the lid cut thirty-six stakes about 15 inches long.

This is the star center shown in Figure 39, but with six groups of six stakes each. I did two rounds of *twining* and then left a space. The ribbon was actually an afterthought. I planned to use a calico print for the pincushion, so originally I left the space to let the print show through. The ribbon makes a handy handle though. So after three more rounds of *twining* over groups of three stakes, I did twelve rounds of *Japanese* weave (*over-two-under-one*). Check often to fit the lid to the bottom. You may need more or fewer rows. Be sure to leave enough room for the border of the lid, which is three rounds, as follows: Round one (using three stakes as one still), Figure 33, under one and up. Round two, Figure 37, over three and down. Round three, Figure 34.

For hinges I used little bits of leather. The handle, as you know, is velvet ribbon.

SCRAP BASKET

The day that I began to put this book to paper, I started cleaning out my desk. Dick, my husband, appeared on the scene several hours later to find me picking up the debris from all over the floor. He announced, "What you need is a scrap basket." Whereupon we both thought a few minutes. It was true! There were no scrap baskets in our entire household (except for the ones with plants living in them). And I've been a basket weaver for many years.

Scrap basket.

Well, I made this one and I like it a lot. I have the perfect plant for it. Funny, though; after I made it, it disappeared. When I found it, it was under my husband's desk, full of scraps!

I wish the picture showed the color texture better. This is one of my more creative basket ideas (it was my friend Andy's idea) and it really looks good. Tie-dyed reed. I used dark brown and chocolate brown, and I dyed the one-pound roll of reed intact and in thirds. In other words, without undoing the reed I stuck it into a pail of hot dye so that a third of it was in the dye. After twenty minutes or so I put another third of it into the other color and left the third third natural.

You will need:

#4 reed
#5 reed

Stakes are #4 reed, and there are twelve of them 68 inches long. And there are twenty-four of them 30 inches long.

With the twelve long stakes and a #4 weaver, do the center (Fig. 31). Go around four times each way, pinching and folding back the weaver.

Then do several rounds of *in-and-out* over groups of three stakes, changing at the start of each round. But here it really makes no matter how you make the bottom. Eventually, I broke down to single stakes with *twining.* When the base was nearly eleven inches across, I did four rounds of *three rod wale* with #5 reed, soaked the whole thing, added one stake to pair up with each other stake, and upsett with three more rounds of *three rod wale.*

The weave up the side is *slewing* with four weavers of #4 reed, changing over two at the start of each round. Halfway up the side I did another round of *three rod wale* with #5 reed but I cannot, now, think why.

The top edge of the basket is five rounds of *three rod wale* with #5 reed, two rounds of *twining,* and then the two-round border (Figs. 33, 37), going outside two and in. The border is worked with two stakes as one.

LAUNDRY BASKET

This basket is very lightweight, yet it is strong enough for laundry. I used #6 half-round for the weaver, which gives it boldness but keeps it light. It is also airy because of the *Colonial* weave. To make the same basket for outdoor work, like picking apples, I would say to use #6 round reed.

On the bottom I had the round side inside, and on the sides the round side outside.

You will need:

1 lb. of #7 reed
2 long strands of #4 reed
(about) 10 strands #6 reed
1 lb. #6 half-round reed
#8 and #3 reed for handles

Cut eight stakes 68 inches long from #7 reed. Do the center

Laundry basket.

(Fig. 31), four rounds, and then break down to single stakes, weaving *Japanese* weave, *over-two-under-one*, for several rounds (about nine).

Cut fifteen stakes 31 inches long and add one to each of the existing stakes, leaving one odd.

Colonial weave fills out the base, which is 14 inches across.

Use four rounds of *three rod wale* with #6 reed for the up-sett. Then the sides are more *Colonial* weave. Three quarters of the way up, I did a round of *three rod wale* with #6 reed and then a couple of rounds before the border.

The border is three rounds. Round one, inside of two and out (Fig. 35). Round two, under two and in. Round three, inside of one and out.

The two hand-sized, handy handles are made with #8 core and roped with #3 reed.

Little things basket.

LITTLE THINGS BASKET

This basket was made in the window of Barclays Bank in Boston where I was demonstrating basketry for my book, *Basic Baskets*. I'm very fond of it.

You will need:

#4 reed for stakes
#2 reed for weavers
Hong Kong Grass, rope, flat or oval reed — you can even use one #4 weaver and one #2 weaver

Fig. 39

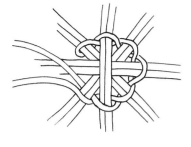

Cut eight stakes of #4 reed and soak them for a few minutes. Soak also three or four weavers of #2 reed. Don't soak the rope or Hong Kong Grass.

Begin with the center (Fig. 39).

Twine around the pairs of stakes four rounds, then break down to single stakes for two more rounds of twining. Now, begin the *double twist* weave (Fig. 20), going back to pairs of stakes, upsetting at the same time. It is a good idea to give each stake a pinch. When the woven sides are about three inches high, work the basic border (Figs. 33, 38), using each pair of stakes as if they were a single stake.

Left: Covered bottle for soy sauce.

Right: Covered detergent bottle.

COVERED BOTTLES

All the mysteries of times before ours, the secrets that die with the dead, are raked out for me to ponder as I begin to write about "covered vessels." I read that the earliest baskets were just knots tied around pottery jugs to help keep them from breaking or to insulate them or to tie them onto the saddles of camels. They say that the earliest pots were leftover build-up on the insides of baskets when the baskets finally wore out. The whole speculation stirs such tender questions in me, and such an awe for my own time and its secrets to our children.

Herein lies my purpose in basketry, cryptic as it is.

Covered bottles are useful now, for insulation, for protection, for carrying, for aesthetics, for gifts. I buy soy sauce by the gallon, so I covered a bottle to have a nice decanter for table use. My liquid dish soap is also wrapped up, just for fun. Where I live there are quantities of rose hips growing. A good cough syrup is rose-hip syrup, made by boiling down their "juice" with honey. That syrup, put up in bottles, is a fine gift. It tastes good on ice cream, too.

Covering bottles is very easy. All you have to do is decide by comparison how many stakes you need for a basket; just approximate the circumference of the bottle. Then you weave the bottom and upsett around the bottle. If you have a bottle that you will eventually want to exchange for a new one, such as a catsup bottle, stop weaving before you close in on the shoulder of the bottle. If you have trouble knowing what to do with extra stakes when you get up around the neck of a bottle, join them up in pairs or threes or fours. If necessary, cut off every other one.

Here is how to make the dark bottle.

You will need:

several strands of #2 reed

Cut twelve stakes 24 inches long. Do the center (Fig. 39). Do *twining* until just before the upsett. Then do *three rod wale* to upsett and until you are ready to leave open space. I did one row of *twining* just to tighten everything up.

The two rows of *twining* there in the middle are called *fitching*. The stakes are arranged as the *fitching* is put on. Then there is more *twining* up around the top; I guess that must be called *fitching*, too. I did a few rounds of *three rod wale*. The border is one round (Fig. 33). Then do two rounds of Figure 34, using all three stakes as one.

To make the covered soap bottle, you will need:

#4 reed
#2 reed
narrow flat oval reed

Cut seven stakes 26 inches long.

The covered soap bottle is done with an oval base, the

Fig. 40

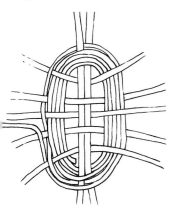

skimpiest base I've ever seen (Fig. 40). Oval bases seem to do best with *randing*. This one is woven with *randing*. Three rounds of *three rod wale* are used to upsett. Then with narrow flat oval reed, weave four rounds of *in-an-out,* changing once each round at the beginning of each round. The main part of the bottle is covered with *wraparound* weave. This is a good weave for fruit baskets. I did four more rounds of *in-and-out* at the top just to balance the bottom. The border is two rounds (Figs. 35, 36).

PLANTERS

When it comes to plants, just about any basket in the world can be used as a holder. My boss puts poinsettias in an enormous antique oak splint basket. If you look closely you'll dis-

Planter.

cover that they are propped up on coffee cans, but they look beautiful.

Fig. 41

One of the problems with plants is drainage. If the basket has to catch the drips, it can quickly get buggy and moldy. So, although I encourage you to use any or all ideas you can to make planters, I have come up with "the ultimate definitive hanging or sitting planter design." Of course, I didn't invent it. I found it. But it solves two problems. And, like anything else, its variations are endless.

The major strength in just about any basket is the stakes (though I must give credit where it is due and say that the weaver and the "weaving" itself have an effect on the strength — my husband wrote a song that goes, "I love you knowing we are more than both of us"). Back to the stakes. I have always loved the way the stakes group together in the middle, then reach up and out to hold something, and then join together again at the rim to hold themselves together.

Fig. 42

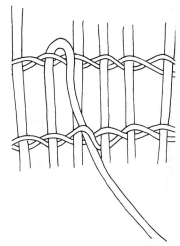

Well, in this basket idea, they go even one step further and provide either a foot for air circulation or a very secure border for hanging.

You will need:

#4 reed
½-inch half-round reed

Cut sixteen stakes, 30 inches long. Soak them and soak four #4 weavers. Soak also two ½-inch half-round weavers.

The center is Figure 41. After the first four rounds I begin twining, breaking down to pairs of stakes that I keep throughout. When the base is about 5½ inches, I upsett with three rounds of *three rod wale*. Then I weave in the half-round to a height of about 4½ inches, using a plain *in-and-out* weave, changing over two once each round. One round of *three rod wale* goes on top.

Fig. 43

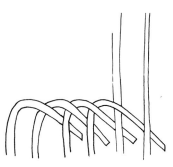

Check to see if the stakes need soaking, then take each pair of stakes through the topmost of the three bottom rounds of *three rod wale* (Fig. 42). Then weave two more rounds of *three rod wale* upside-down onto those stakes and work the simple one-step border (Fig. 43). Trim the stakes.

Onion basket.

ONION STORAGE BASKET

The first year I gave baskets as Christmas presents, they mostly looked like this one. I had just discovered that chair cane woven over #4 reed makes a somewhat flexible form that continues to intrigue me. I like the way the container adapts to accommodate that which it is asked to contain. That year I called them "banana baskets." Now I hang this one on the wall and use it for onions, so I call it an "onion basket." It looks more like an onion anyway.

You will need:

#4 reed
medium chair cane

Cut sixteen stakes 45 inches long and one bye stake 25 inches long. Soak them a few minutes, and soak five weavers. The cane needn't be soaked for this.

Arrange the sixteen stakes as in Figure 32. Leave the bye stake out for now.

Weave around four times, pinch, and go back in the other direction for four rounds. Pinch again and go back in the original direction four more rounds.

Insert the bye stake right at the start of the next round and break down to pairs of stakes (use the bye stake singly).

Work *in-and-out* weave approximately eight rounds, then change to cane and break down again to single stakes. Work this weave approximately ten inches.

The border is done in two rounds. It is just like the basic border, but inside of two and then outside two (Figs. 35, 37).

The basket can be finished as is by clipping off the ends. The finish in the picture is made in the same way as an interior ledge for a lid, like the sewing basket, or just for design, like the laundry hamper. I made this ledge by cutting off one of each pair. Don't cut the bye stake. Then I wove eight rounds on the remaining stake ends with a #4 weaver.

Finally, I did the simple border (Fig. 43) and trimmed the ends.

The handle is a loop of leather.

HAMPER

This hamper is made in three stages. First, the bottom is made and a border woven on. Then the side stakes are inserted down through the base, one on each side of each base stake, and a foot border woven with their bottom ends. Then the lid is added. The purpose of these first two steps is twofold. First, they raise the actual base off the floor a little, allowing for circulation, and, second, the stakes you are working with are of a manageable length. I am not convinced that either reason is really valid, especially when you're working with reed. Feet can be added as they were on the rucksack. And reed is *almost* easier to handle in long pieces. But I want to share the idea, as there are times when it is useful.

You will need:

#4 reed
#5 reed
#6 reed
fiber rush

Fig. 44

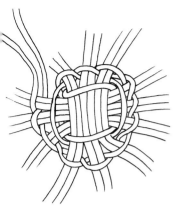

For the base, cut twelve stakes 28 inches long. Do the center (Fig. 44). Break down to pairs and then later break down to single stakes. The weave is *twining* all the way. The base measures 15 inches across. The border for the base is the two-round border (Figs. 33, 38).

The sides are made on forty-seven stakes 30 inches long. These stakes are inserted through the base, between the last row of weaving and the border, one on each side of each base stake minus one, making an odd number to accommodate *in-and-out* weave. On the bottom of the base, a foot border is woven with the ends of the stakes just inserted. It is a two-round border (Figs. 33, 38).

The sides are just *in-and-out* all the way, except for one round of *three rod wale*.

Hamper.

At the top edge is a complex combination of borders. The first is shown in Figure 33. Then, Figure 37, over four and back in. On the ends inside, I wove nine more rows of *in-and-out*. Then another border (Figs. 33, 38), over three and in. Then again, weave on these ends to make a rim for the lid. Weave three rounds of *three rod wale* with #2 weaver, then one more border round (Fig. 43).

The lid is made with eighteen stakes of #6 reed. Cut the stakes 26 inches long. The center is Figure 41, arranged with three groups of four and one group of six, which I put on the top. I did seven rounds and bent the weaver back for four rounds, breaking down to pairs of stakes. Then I bent the weaver back again for three more rounds in the original direction. I wove two rounds of *three rod wale* and then *in-and-out* until the lid was about an inch shy of fitting all around. Then I did two rounds of *three rod wale*. The border is Figures 33 and 37, except: over three and down.

FRUIT BASKET

This basket is fun and easy to make. It's good for fruit because it lets air circulate. You will need an awl and some

Fruit basket.

Fig. 45 Scallop border.

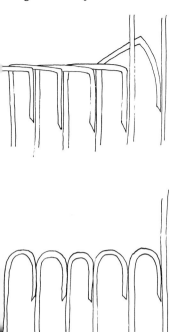

round-nosed pliers. I made this with #4 reed. I bet it would be real nice made of honeysuckle.

You will need:

some #4 reed
an awl
round-nosed pliers

Cut twelve stakes 38 inches long. The center is Figure 39, except, of course, there are three stakes in each group of stakes. The weave is *twining*. After four rounds, break down to pairs of stakes and gently shape the bowl. I did twelve rounds. The bowl is 9½ inches in diameter.

Now stop and soak the whole thing for ten minutes. Then, working the scallop border (Fig. 45), feed each pair of stakes through ten rows and back out.

Now again, with *twining*, weave the foot. I did six rounds altogether. Then, again work the scallop border (Fig. 45) and trim.

LETTUCE WASHER

Isn't this silly? But believe me, it really works. If you grow your own greens and can go outside for a minute while fixing salad, you will really appreciate this. Put the washed lettuce leaves in the basket, go outside, grasp both handles, and swing your arm around and around from the shoulder. If you are interested in the exercise, change hands and do it on that side. In a jiffy all the water droplets are gone and the lettuce is ready to serve.

Lettuce washer.

Once you get the reeds cut for stakes, this project only takes about half an hour to make, including handles.

Fig. 46

You will need:

#2 reed

Cut sixteen stakes 30 inches long. I did a cockamamie version of the center (Fig. 46), with eight stakes crossing eight stakes. Then I twined away, eventually breaking down to pairs of stakes. Up at the border edge, I let the rows get close together. The border is the trac border (Fig. 47).

The handles are each made from four pieces of #2 reed cut about 28 inches long. They are twisted together and "tied on," as shown in Figure 27.

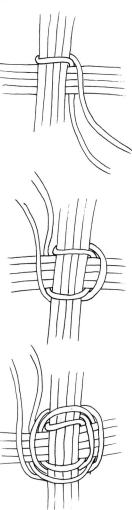

SILVERWARE HOLDERS

The reed is dyed gray because I thought it would resemble pewter. Actually, six months later, it looks more brown than anything. You can see that I made different finishings on these. I did that for you, because this is a book and I wanted to offer as many ideas as possible. You, of course, can make them all alike or as different as you wish. Even the shapes are arbitrary. I took my bunch of knives that we use most every day, put them on a piece of paper, and drew around them. Then I did the same with the forks, spoons, tablespoons, and chopsticks. These are the things I wash most often, and that, of course, is why a basket is so practical. The silverware can be plunked in and left until you want to use it. Even the baskets can be washed every so often.

One pound of #2 reed will make a lot more than five of these.

You will need:

Fig. 47 Trac border.

#2 reed (dyed or natural, again, as you wish)

All the baskets are made essentially the same way, and there's no reason why they can't *all* be the same size and shape. So first, the general recipe; afterward will come the specifics for the others.

Cut eight stakes, each 20 inches long. Then cut sixteen

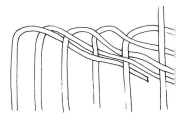

Silverware holders.

stakes, each 10 inches long. Soak them, and soak eight to ten weavers.

With the eight 20-inch stakes, do center Figure 46.

Then begin *twining* and break down to pairs of stakes. Work this way for about six rounds.

Now, insert one 10-inch stake beside each stake. Use an awl if you need to make a little space in the weaving. Also, it helps to cut on the diagonal the end of the stake to be inserted.

Break down again to pairs of stakes and do the *twining* weave, gently shaping the upsett. Work the basket to the desired height.

The border on the knife basket is my favorite. It reminds me of a handknit sweater with the cuff rolled up. That's almost what I did. I turned the well-soaked stakes back down on themselves and wove eleven rows. Then I cut off one of each pair of stakes and worked one round of *three rod wale*. The basket is finished with the simple border (Figs. 33, 38).

The handle is the one in Figure 26. I did it with a pair of reeds, however, and it was easier, quicker, and neater, I believe, than it would have been had I tried to get the same thickness with a single reed.

Before working the border on the fork basket, be sure to soak the stakes if they need it. Count down eight rows of weaving (or the desired number of rows) and, using an awl, lift the weave (just in that row) and thread the stakes down through it. Then work any old border you like. I did two rounds of Figure 34 and ended by taking each end back to the inside, where I trimmed it so that the nearest stake held it inside.

I did the chopsticks basket the same way as the knife basket but with only four rows woven after the top was turned down. Then, for the border, I worked the simple border (Figs. 33, 38), with both stakes in each pair intact, used as one.

The tablespoon basket border, as you can see, is simply eight rows of *twining* woven after the turn down, and the ends of the stakes are trimmed randomly.

The spoon basket is one round of simple border (Fig. 33) and then my dubious invented border (Fig. 34). I say dubious for two reasons. Everything else I think I invented I eventually discover in some old book or basket or other. Also, this

Chopsticks basket.

border is dubiously secure, unless it is done at least two or three rounds. In this basket it is worked with pairs of stakes as one, and it is worked three rounds. Care must be taken to finish each round before beginning the next. What I mean is that when you get to the last stake in the round, tuck it in where it goes to make it look just like the others. Do not simply begin the next round with it. The reasons to be careful are neatness and symmetry, which I do not usually care a fig about. As a teacher, I have found it more important to encourage people to make the basket anyway and not to worry about perfection. Now, of course, I am not there with you to sense which angle to stress. You will know how to use my remarks. I found that for myself, however (and this book *is* something of a record of my paths), I want to know how to make things neat and right for some baskets while in others I want to highlight natural shapes with my natural disregard for perfection.

BERRY BASKET

This will hold enough blueberries for a generous pie. You will need:

Berry basket.

#5 reed for stakes
#2 reed for weavers
one 20-inch piece of large handle reed or three 20-inch pieces of #5

Fig. 48

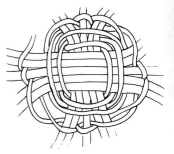

Cut and soak ten stakes of #5 reed 24 inches long and one bye stake 12 inches long. You'll need lots of weavers. I find it's always best to soak a few at a time.

Do the center shown in Figure 48. The figure shows two rounds around groups of five stakes. Then it shows one round of a two, one, two breakdown. Do a second two, one, two round, then break down to one, one, one, one, one. Weave the base to a diameter of 5 inches. Now you can cut a point on the bye stake and insert it alongside one of the stakes. Do four or five rounds of *three rod wale* to fix the upsett. Then weave *in-and-out* with two weavers as one to a height of 5 inches.

The border is two rounds (Figs. 33, 37).

The handle I used should have been carved down a little more. It pushed the basket a bit out of shape. The way to make the handle is illustrated in Figure 29.

HAT

This hat is a definitive example of the style of presentation I offer in this book. So many of the specifics presented are, in the broader sense, truly meaningless. I speak specifically in my directions, but I do not expect you to follow my specifics blindly.

I always do whatever I feel like at the moment when making baskets, using my best judgment, of course. I usually do what electricity does and take the path of least resistance. I encourage you to do the same.

My main concern with the hat was how to get the little cut-off ends out of the way. That was a problem with the baby basket, too. I didn't like this solution for the baby basket, but it does seem a good answer for the hat.

You will need:

#2 reed

Cut and soak six 35-inch stakes and twenty-four 18-inch

Hat.

stakes. Soak also several weavers. For a larger hat with a broader brim, use eight at 35 inches and thirty-three at 18 inches. For a doll's hat, four stakes and 17 inches are enough.

Again, you can use any center arrangement. I used the one in Figure 46. After about twelve rows of *twining*, insert one of the shorter stakes along *each* side of each stake. The extra one goes in anywhere, making one group of four stakes. Then, using four weavers as one, do *in-and-out* weave, changing at the start of each round, for five rounds. Break down to single stakes and a single weaver and continue *in-and-out* weave for about 3 inches. Then return to the four weaver *in-and-out* weave for at least three rounds. Twelve rounds of *in-and-out* with a single weaver complete the weaving.

The border is the same idea as was used in Figure 42. Working with nice wet stakes, instead of threading each stake through a row of weaving, I threaded it right through from the underside of the hat to the topside. I then did two rounds of my "invented" border (Fig. 34), after which I took each end back to the inside, did the two-round border (Figs. 33, 38). As if that weren't enough, I tucked the ends back through to the outside and there trimmed them off.

To finish the hat in a way that it will stay on in the Nantucket wind, I tacked a kerchief inside. Ribbons could also have been used. Also, hats can be trimmed with anything. My mother-in-law made a really cute doll's hat trimmed with ribbon and cloth flowers.

DOLL'S CHAIR AND TABLE

These are both made the same way, which can be described as joining two baskets by a common bottom, one upside-down, the other "upside-up." This basic concept can be used in lots of ways, and the furniture itself can be made in any number of sizes and shapes. I, of course, used my family's most popular dolls for size.

You will need:

#2 reed

Jim setting the table.

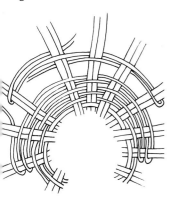

Fig. 49 Doll's chair.

For the chair, cut twelve stakes 20 inches long. Using *twining*, do the center in Figure 46, with six stakes crossing six. Break down to two, two, and two after the first round. After about eight rounds, or when the "seat" is big enough, begin weaving the *in-and-out* weave back and forth,

a) still using two stakes as one
b) weaving on nine pairs of stakes
c) upsetting those nine pair
d) leaving the rest alone (Fig. 49)

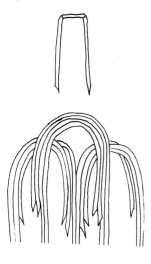

Fig. 50 Doll's chair.

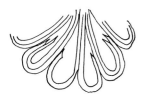

The table legs are eight pieces cut about 20 inches long. They are soaked, pinched, and inserted through the tabletop in the same way as the chair "legs." They can then, of course, be woven in the same way as the legs. In my never-ending delight for trying things out, I did (as you see in the picture) two *very* loose rows of my "invented" border (Fig. 34).

Then I gathered up the ends and wove nine rounds of *twining* to flare out a practical base. The border is the scallop border (Fig. 50).

Begin the base by cutting eight 12-inch stakes and soaking them. Then pinch them twice about a quarter of an inch apart so that they will bend easily. Now, insert them down through the woven chair seat so that they "straddle" the stakes.

Twelve rows, more or less, of *twining* will make a nice stand for the chair. As you weave, flare the base out somewhat so that the chair will stand properly. The base is finished with a simple border (Figs. 33, 38).

The tabletop is much simpler than the chair, though it begins the same way.

Cut and soak eight stakes 12 inches long. Do the center (Fig. 46) with the *twining* weave. Break down each group of eight to four and four the second round. After four rounds of that, break down again to two, two, two, and two. Weave to a diameter of 5 inches, then break down once again to single stakes. Upsett to make an edge to the table, then work a simple two-round border as in Figures 33 and 38.

CASSEROLE BASKET

If you go to potluck suppers once in a while, you'll get some use from one of these. I use this basket at our own table, too.

You will need:

Hong Kong Grass
#2 reed

Cut the stakes (twelve of them in this case) about 4 to 6 inches longer on each side than the span around the casserole. This one needs stakes cut 18 inches.

The center is Figure 46, with six stakes crossing six stakes. I did *twining* for a few rounds, establishing a breakdown to pairs of stakes. As soon as there was room, I began the *double twist* weave with one weaver of Hong Kong Grass breaking down to single weavers as soon as there was enough space.

The border is one round (Fig. 33) and then three rounds (Fig. 34). Then, to add "weight" to the look of the border, I wrapped it once around with another weaver.

The two handles are the simple handles shown in Figure 26.

LAMP

Here is another example of something that can be made in a number of shapes. The lamp is fashioned from an empty wine bottle, a "make-it-yourself-lamp-kit," and an old lamp shade. I used the lamp shade because it really is necessary to diffuse the light. Basket weaving alone is not enough. I also used the lamp shade because the little clip makes it easy to use. The weave is predominately *Japanese* (*over-two-under-one*) with *over-four-under-one* making the spiral on the neck.

You will need:

#2 reed

Cut and soak seventeen 40-inch stakes and several weavers. Sixteen of the stakes are used to do the center (Fig. 30). The extra stake is pinched and folded in half, to be inserted as a pair of bye stakes as soon as possible. I went four rounds one way, four the other way, inserted the bye stake, and began *in-and-out* weave.

When the base is *almost* as big as the bottom of the bottle (one round smaller), do a round of *three rod wale* and break down to single stakes. Three more rounds of *three rod wale* accomplish the upsett. I then started weaving with a single weaver, *Japanese* weave (*under-one-over-two*), including the wire from the lamp on the inside. Because of the number of stakes I had, the *over-two-under-one* weave made a left-sloping spiral.

At the "shoulder" of the bottle, I did one row of *three rod wale*. I do not think that in this case it served any particular use. When I used it on the bottom, it really helped even out the spacing.

In order to close in around the bottle, I joined the stakes into pairs and wove *Japanese* weave again. This time the slant seemed to go to the right.

At the base of the neck, I cut off one of each pair and began *over-four-under-one*, which gave me that thick spiral effect. I really like that.

As a finishing touch at the top, I did seven rounds of *three rod wale*. *Three rod wale* is great for shaping. And I really used it here as a kind of frame for the other weaving texture

Lamp.

going on between the bottom and top. The finish is the simple two-round border (Figs. 33, 38).

The shade is made with the same center as the base, but in order to keep the spaces small I used only eight stakes, four pair to start.

Cut eight stakes 30 inches long. Then cut eighteen stakes 15 inches long. Begin with four rounds one way, four rounds back, and four more the first way. Then add the extra stakes, one beside each one already in. There are two extra, which I just put in along with two others. This seems unreasonable, but I had a reason. I wanted to keep the texture of the weave as close to the base as possible, so I wanted to have the stakes about the same distance apart most of the time.

The whole top is *Japanese* weave, weaving right around the lamp shade. Actually, the only thing that is holding the lamp shade in its woven cover is that the cover is so snug.

The lamp shade border is Figure 33, round one, inside one and out, and round two, Figure 37, over two and back in.

SOFT CARRIERS

Left: Soft red bag.

Middle: Striped soft carrier.

Right: Brown soft carrier.

When I want to get involved in a long-term project of a week or two, I make soft woven baskets. They are a real change from reed work because of color possibilities and soft texture.

They also illustrate that the whole is stronger than its weavers or stakes.

I used *twining* almost exclusively. With a soft warp, it's almost impossible to get anywhere with a single weaver. Also, *twining* makes possible an easy design, which I just love (Fig. 51).

There is one other weave that fascinates me, especially with soft weaving. Indeed, it cannot be done with other than a soft weaver (Fig. 14). It gives a stretchy quality to the bag. It is, however, a "tighter" weave than *twining*, so it will affect the shape of the work. I call it *wraparound* weave.

I think that a specific recipe for soft work would be rather useless. Follow one of the oldest "rules" of basketry, "Use what's available," and experiment.

I recommend the center in Figure 52, which also shows how to add stakes. Stakes have to be added regularly until the bottom is its full size. All you have to do to upsett is stop adding stakes and keep on weaving. I always pack in the weaving every so often.

The red carrier has jute stakes (approximately 4.5 m.m.). The weaver is three strands of yarn together. One strand is heavy wool rug yarn and two strands are mohair bouclé yarn with variations in the color. This gives the bag a lovely soft texture that I highlighted (though very subtly) with a row of glass beads about an inch and a half from the top. I wove *twining* weave all the way. The center is shown in Figure 52, and I added stakes for a total of eighty. I did the two-round border (Figs. 33, 38), with the help of a large-eyed needle. Then, also with the needle, I took each end back inside the weaving alongside a stake. The handle was made like my bike carryall. I simply tied on four lengths of jute and then wove in yarn to fill them up (*in-and-out* weave). Overall measurements are 8 inches high by 7 inches wide.

The striped bag is mostly of jute (approximately 5.25 m.m.). I used yarn as decoration. The border is a trac border (Fig. 47). It measures approximately 6 inches high by 9 inches wide.

The brown basket is one of my most favorites of all time. I took extra care making it. It is about 10 inches wide. I used special heavy jute (about $7.00 worth). There are sixty-eight

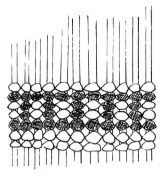

Fig. 51 Patterns can be developed using colors.

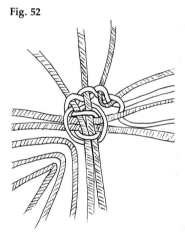

Fig. 52

stakes around. The weavers are hand-spun Greek goat hair, hand-spun lamb's wool, and chenille. I did the top 2 inches of weaving with the wool because it is softer. I did a border of knots. Then I wove a strap of wool chenille, which I sewed on over the "ends" of the border. The handle is all wool, *in-and-out* weave.

VIII Oval Baskets

I didn't make oval baskets much until I decided to do this book. I just wasn't intrigued. But when I set myself the specific task of a "useful" basket book, I began to appreciate a funny thing. Oval baskets are easier to use. When it comes to actual lifting and carrying, oval's easier. I even learned that the hard way with my first attempt at a rucksack or backpack. I made it oval, but not oval enough, and for town use it was hazardous.

When designing an oval basket, it is helpful to analyze what you're after. An oval basket is a circle, cut in half and moved apart a given distance. The stakes in between essentially maintain their relative distances from each other. So, for instance, if you decide on a basket with stakes about an inch apart at the ends, be sure to use enough long-wise stakes. Then space the stakes down the middle an inch apart.

Another point about oval bases in general is that they are very hard to keep flat. Not only can they ripple, they can wrack. I have read that one should never *twine* or *wale* on an oval bottom. I've also read that you can *twine* and *wale* all you want as long as you go backward as much as forward (*chain pairing* or *arrow* weaving). My prejudice is toward following the "never" rule. But I don't ever believe in such absolutes, so I will offer this advice: "I think you'll do better if you do mostly *randing* on oval bases."

Also, you will find many of these baskets made on split-stake bases. That is to say, some of the stakes are split and the others are fed through them. This helps to keep the bottom

Oval bases.

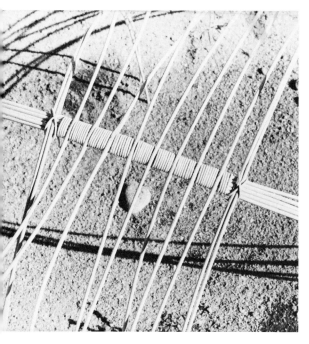

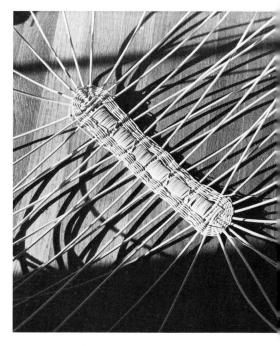

flat and helps to hold everything. My favorite oval base, which I found easy to hold, is the one on the baby basket and picnic basket, and they are not split. So here is a variety of techniques accomplishing a variety of tasks.

Fig. 53

SOAP DISH

This is an open oval base. It is hard to keep the dish from having spaces, so you can't use it for a pocketbook. But you can use this general idea for fruit, bread, or soap.

You will need:

#2 reed

Since this is so small, there is no need to differentiate between the long stakes and the short stakes. Cut sixteen stakes 12 inches long and two more for bye stakes 5 inches long. Set the bye stakes aside. Arrange the sixteen stakes as in Figure 53. The weaver goes three times around in one direction, then pinched, it bends back and goes the other way three times. The end stakes are then broken down to pairs. Insert the bye stakes for that. Use *in-and-out* weave all the way. When the base is about 4 inches long and 3¼ inches wide, pinch the stakes and upsett. The border is a trac border (Fig. 47).

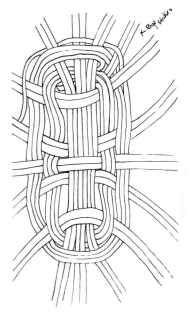

Soap dish.

Cracker basket.

CRACKER BASKET

Fig. 54

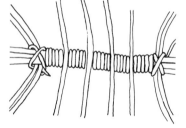

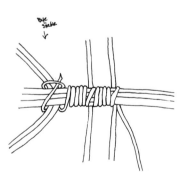

You will need:

#4 reed
#2 reed

Cut six stakes 22 inches, eight stakes 15 inches, and one stake 8 inches for a bye stake. Carefully make a slit in the centers of the eight 15-inch stakes and thread the six long stakes through them. The binding is done by beginning at one end with one end of a long weaver (Fig. 54). The whole base is *in-and-out* weave. Insert the bye stake by a shoulder stake so that the ends can be broken down in two stages to pairs and then to single stakes.

When the base is approximately 8 inches long and 4 inches wide, upsett. I did one round of *three rod wale*, eight rounds of *randing*, and another of *three rod wale*. Then I did five rounds of *slewing* with four weavers and some *three rod waling* just before the border.

74

The border is two rounds. Round one is Figure 35, inside two and back out. Round two is Figure 55, under three and back inside.

Fig. 55

MAIL BASKET

I saw this weave on a flower basket. I think it's rather fun. You will see that I made this basket before I figured out the trick with designing oval bases. I thought I would need more stakes along the front and back, but since I didn't, I left them as pairs. Also, I must comment on my seeming error, which is apparent here. I changed the weave over one, after two rounds, and then put it back for the top round. Since this basket is made on an even number of stakes, the weave need not, however, be changed.

Baskets like this are also useful on a bathroom wall (you can make two or three baskets alike) to hold hairbrushes and shampoo, etc.

You will need:

#4 reed
#2 reed

Cut nine stakes 24 inches long and five 28 inches long. Make a slit in the middle of the shorter stakes and thread the longer ones through them. The weave is *arrow,* or one round of "S" twist *twining* and one round "Z" twist. I found this

Mail basket.

cumbersome to accomplish and not completely successful in keeping the base flat.

When the base measured 9¼ inches by 2¼ inches, I did two rounds of *three rod wale* with #4 reed, one "S" twist, and one "Z" twist. Then I did the X weave up the sides to a height of 5½ inches. Another two rounds of *three rod wale* with #2 reed are under the border. The border is shown in Figures 35 and 37.

Sally's sock basket.

SALLY'S SOCK BASKET

When my friend Sally went to England, she entrusted me with the care of her baskets. I grew especially fond of one in particular, partly because it is such a sturdy thing for such a pretty thing and partly because it solved graciously a growing problem I faced: socks. I don't mind washing clothes and I like hanging them out. Bringing them in is fun, but my interest begins to wane when it comes to folding and sorting. Socks to me are just about the last straw. They never have partners. But now, thanks to the wonder of a humble container, all clean socks that don't easily find their way to the drawer sit happily in one spot. What is truly appealing is that when a problem is solved it really ceases to be. No one even misses the problem. Socks are no longer nasty to me. If the basket gets too full, there are usually some pairs lurking inside, or at least a few cleaning rags.

When Sally returned from England, I had to make a copy of her basket. Here it is.

It is made on a "slath," or a separate bottom. The slath is a characteristic of willow basketry, which takes advantage of the stouter pieces of willow rods for the bottom and still allows enough flexibility for the upsett. Willow rods are also known as Sally rods, as I mentioned in the discussion of hedgerow materials. I can recommend this type of bottom because it is flat. The only concern I have is that the bottom must be fully woven and the upsett distinct. The side stakes must be inserted all the way. You do not want to pick up the basket and have the bottom stay on the floor.

You will need:

Fig. 56

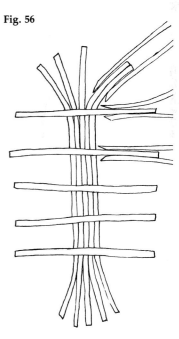

#6 reed for bottom and handles
#4 reed for side stakes and upsett
#6 half-round reed for weaver and handle wrapper
#2 reed to weave bottom

Cut five pieces of #6 reed 11 inches long; they will later be trimmed but I always like to have a little leeway. Then cut five pieces of #6 reed 7 inches long. And you will need a bye stake, or you will need to keep two stakes as one at one end, just for the base. This second alternative is indicated in Figure 56. Split the centers of each of the shorter stakes with a very sharp knife and thread the five longer ones through.

Now weave *in-and-out* weave with a single weaver, breaking down the ends right away to two, one, two on one end and on the other end. After a few rounds, these break down respectively to one, one, one, one, one and two, one, one, one.

When the weaving measures 8½ inches by 5 inches, do one round of *three rod wale* with #6 reed. Trim the stakes very close to this row of weaving.

Cut thirty-eight stakes about 20 inches long and insert them one on each side of each stake in the base (except for the pair).

Fig. 57

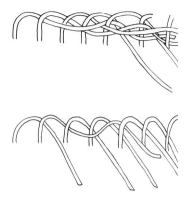

Pinch these stakes and upsett them with another round of *three rod wale* using #6 reed. The side stakes are used in pairs.

Weave the sides *in-and-out* weave with #6 half-round reed.

The border, worked with pairs of stakes, is round one (Fig. 57).

BREAD BASKET

You will need:

#6 half-round reed
#4 reed
#2 reed

Cut five stakes 35 inches long and twelve stakes 28 inches long. Slit the shorter stakes in the center and thread the longer ones through. This is begun at one end and wrapped to the other, as in Figure 54. After just a few rounds of *in-and-out* with a change at the start of each round, begin the *belle-fonte* weave (Fig. 16), *over-three-under-one*. For the base, this weave is worked with the bottom facing the weaver.

The upsett is two rounds of *three rod wale*, *arrow* fashion, or what is known as "chain waling." Then, *bellefonte* done with #6 half-round. The weaver works it *inside-three-outside-one*.

Bread basket.

Bread basket.

Another chain wale catches in those straying stakes.

The border is: Round one: Figure 35, inside two and out. Round two, Figure 37, over two and back in. Round three, Figure 34.

RUCKSACK

I hadn't used a backpack until I made one for this book. I had intended to call it a city backpack.

I was working about a mile and a quarter from my house and trying to get exercise, so I made it a habit to walk to and from work. Thus, I got to test out three different packs. The first was too round — it made me self-conscious. Maybe I wouldn't have felt that way if I were used to packs. But I also felt it was too easy for anyone else to lift something out of it, and that made me feel defensive. So, I discarded that style and made one I really love. The Hong Kong Grass basket.

Well, I felt good with this one. I must say I was immediately won over to the backpack way of carrying. So I used the Hong Kong Grass pack for a while, until one day I had both a half gallon of milk and a bottle of wine to tote home. Unfortunately, the pack itself was already heavy, and real weight inside made it a drag. Back to the drawing board.

By now I was intrigued with the challenge of a flat, semi-cone shape to be done with reed.

I decided I would want lots of stakes to flare out the ends. I used eighteen lengthwise stakes and only twelve crosswise, grouped into three groups of four each.

You will need:

#2 reed
#4 reed
flat 1-inch reed
3 wooden drawer pulls
a soft tie-belt

Cut thirty stakes 40 inches long.

Figure 58 shows how to hold everything together. Figure 59 shows the breakdown, which is in groups. The actual count is indicated. After only a few rounds of *in-and-out* weave, I upsett with two rounds of *three rod wale* with #4 reed. Then I broke down to pairs on the ends (the crossways stakes I kept as four for a while) as shown in the photo on page 80.

The dark band is *three rod wale*, but the rest is all *in-and-out*.

The border is round one as shown in Figure 33. Round two is Figure 34, and round three is Figure 38.

I "finished" the basket with two coats of polyurethane. The "strap" is one terry-cloth sash threaded through. I can pull up on the knot and wear it like a shoulder bag, which I like because in stores it is more comfortable that way.

The other clever little feature of this backpack is that it has three feet, so it "stands" by itself. These are drawer pulls. I put several layers of leather on each side of the basket to act as washers. The screws, which are sold with the drawer pulls, are a little too long. This means that the feet are a little loose. If you want feet that fit, ask the hardware-store person to sell you shorter screws that will fit the drawer pull.

Rucksack.

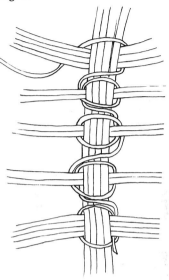

Fig. 58

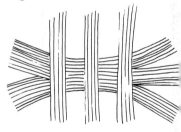

Fig. 59 Rucksack breakdown.

Bike basket and carryall.

Bike basket.

BIKE BASKET

I love my bike and I use it a lot, so I wanted it to have a good-looking basket. I am also inclined to do several things at once. So I park it and lock it someplace and go around to do my several things. I wanted to make a basket that would hold my carryall so I could carry all my things with me.

This basket fills my needs. I was given the pieces of ash splint that are the side weavers. They are especially pretty.

You will need:

#6 reed
#2 reed
#4 reed
flat reed or ash splints or other weaver
two leather straps to fasten the basket to the bicycle

Cut six stakes 35 inches long.

The center is Figure 54. Then the entire base is woven with *in-and-out* weave, changing at the beginning of each round. I broke down the ends right at the start. The #4 weaver is for design. Then I did some packing at each end to make the oval longer. The upsett is *three rod wale,* one round, done with #4.

The sides are *Colonial* weave, or *over-two-under-two,* with a change of over three at the start of each round.

A few rounds of *three rod wale,* and then the border is Figures 33 and 37 and next continues on the inside over two more and back out.

GARDEN BASKET

This basket reminds me of my grandma's kitchen.
You will need:

#6 reed
#2 reed
1 hank of sash cord (50 feet or 16⅔ yards)
#6 half-round reed
some cotton twine for handle
2 porcelain drawer pulls

Cut sixteen stakes 30 inches long and six stakes 40 inches long.

The center is Figure 54. I wove at first with #2 reed, *in-and-out* weave, changing at the beginning of each round. I wove the bottom with the round side of the #6 half-round up.

The border is Figure 35 and two rounds of Figure 34.

Garden basket.

Picnic basket.

PICNIC BASKET

You will need:

#6 reed
#4 reed
#2 reed, just a few strands for the center
1 piece #10 for handle
1 long strip #6 half-round for wrapping the handle
Hong Kong Grass

Cut six stakes 50 inches long and twenty stakes 45 inches long. The center is Figure 58. I always have trouble deciding how to accomplish an *in-and-out* weave on an oval bottom. This one is a good example of some of my tricky solutions.

Don't worry about them. The simplest thing to do is change once each round.

I did two rounds of *three rod wale* at the upsett. In order to have an uneven number of stakes, I kept two together. I even kept them together to weave the border.

The sides are woven with Hong Kong Grass, *in-and-out* weave.

The border is Figure 35, inside-two-and-out, then on top of three, as in Figure 34, under one and back in.

LAUNDRY BASKET

My idea here was to make a large version of Sally's sock basket, on a separate base.

You will need:

#8 reed for base
#4 reed
#6 reed
flat oval reed ¼ inch narrow

Cut three stakes 21 inches long. Cut six stakes 12 inches long. Cut also four shoulder stakes 6 inches long. Pierce the centers of the six short stakes and thread the long stakes through.

The base is Figure 60, simple *in-and-out*. I went three rounds, changed by going under two for three more rounds. Then I changed again, and again went three rounds. At this point I added shoulder stakes, one at each corner, and broke down to single stakes, changing every round. When the base was big enough, 17½ inches by 10 inches, I trimmed off the excess stake length.

Cut sixty-seven stakes of #6 reed. I inserted one stake on each side of each base stake, down the sides, and two stakes at each side of the shoulders and ends. See Figure 61 for the arrangement, and note the arrow that points out the omission of one stake to leave us an odd number.

Next, I did one round of *four rod wale*. Then I soaked the whole thing, pinched each stake, and did a second round of *four rod wale*.

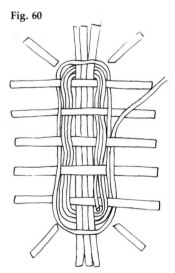

Fig. 60

Fig. 61

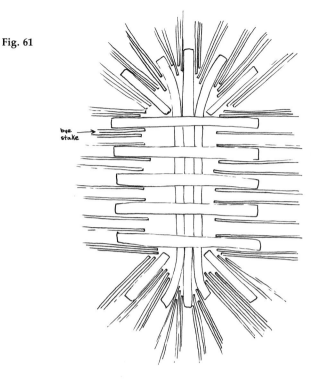

bye
stake

The sides were a breeze. This whole basket seemed easy. *In-and-out* with flat oval reed.

There is a round of *four rod wale* at the top. The border is Figure 35, over four on the outside and back in, over one more on the inside and out.

The two little handles are wrapped with #6 half-round.

BABY BASKET

I've been asked how to make a baby basket many times. Grandmothers-to-be, aunts-to-be, and mothers themselves have pondered the task. I put off attempting to answer until Holly Brenizer, one of my bravest students, ventured into the unknown. She did it. And when I asked her, she came over with it and let me photograph her and it. The basket she made just melted my resistance. I had another friend who would soon need one, so I flew off into a whirl of activity, which you see pictured here.

Holly's basket cost her about twenty dollars to make. She

Holly Brenizer and her baby basket.

A breadboard to work on.

Ready to be soaked.

Getting started.

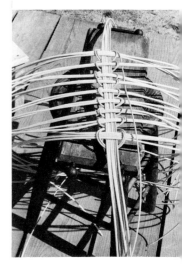

The bottom takes shape.

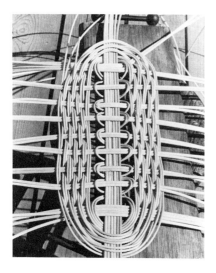

Soaking.

The border that I rejected because of its sharp edges.

Filling in.

The shape of the "bonnet."

lined it with bright red calico, included in the cost, as well as some batting, which she covered for a little mattress.

I looked in all my books for dimensions. Holly's basket measured 29 inches by 17 inches by 10 inches. My books varied, but the range was 26 to 33 inches long, 12 to 18 inches wide, and 8 to 14 inches high. After I was finished, I found an English willow baby basket in a store for thirty-five dollars. It is a standardized style commissioned by the government for use by its employees' families. It is very sturdy and lightweight, being of willow, and its overall dimensions are the largest.

I decided not to make my basket too large, because I wanted it to be useful as a car bed, or, simply, easy to carry. My decision may have shortened the length of time the basket could be used, but a crib basket is only good for a few months anyway. It may make no difference. Anyway, the whole task of making this basket was delightful, and you can see the basket in use. Holly's basket has also been used well.

The second try, completed.

Morgen Van Voorst, about thirty hours old.

You will notice that the finished basket is not the same as in the photo. The first one I made was just not right. I felt it was too small, and for some reason I could not find a satisfactory resolution for the stake ends. So I started over and have given the recipe for my second basket. You will also see that I did one border that was practical but ugly to me, so it got changed.

You will need:

a pound of #6 reed
#4 reed
#6 half-round reed
Hong Kong Grass or flat reed

Holly's basket is done with #6, #4, and flat reed on the sides.

Cut eight stakes 6½ feet long and thirty-two stakes 5½ feet long.

I did the same center shown in the photos on page 87, but this time I used *eight* long stakes instead of six. Again, I used four stakes at each shoulder, but twelve pairs of stakes crossing the middle for additional length. I worked carefully, making sure all the pieces were centered as I began weaving round and round. The round-and-round weaving responded to being pushed back in toward the center.

After soaking in the sink I used #6 reed to upsett with three rounds of *three rod wale*. Then I did *Colonial* weave up the sides. The rows of *three rod wale* are for extra strength, but I've finally convinced myself they're not necessary.

The hood, or bonnet end, is not necessary either, and here's where I ran into a variety of muddy experiments. The procedure is clearer on the first basket. I did want to do a hood, because it looks so right. I copied Holly's method directly. The Hong Kong Grass could be omitted, or the space could be filled in with ribbon; use anything soft and really flexible.

Now I had ended up weaving on pairs of stakes. If you want the basket bigger, weave on the stakes singly from the upsett on and allow the sides to flare out. I ended up by cutting off one of each pair of stakes. Then I did two rounds of *three rod wale* to be sure the cutoff ends were well protected. The border I used finally was Figure 33, Figure 38, over one and out, and Figure 34.

"CANOE" BASKET

This basket represents an idea. I have often seen and admired pictures of a certain type of Pomo Indian basket, shaped like a canoe and decorated with cut shells and feathers. It is made by a coiling technique. The shape is achieved essentially by upsetting the sides before the ends, though it is not called upsetting and since it starts with a circle there are no sides or ends until you make them.

So this oval-shaped basket is actually a round-bottomed basket, included here to share this idea: "Just about *any* shape can be made; there are no limits but those you set yourself."

I do not mean to disparage limits, as such. I have carefully

"Canoe" basket.

set limits for myself, and they are often very helpful. One of them is that I never take orders for specific baskets. I have well established that I cannot make a "living wage" out of the hours I spend weaving baskets. In other words, making baskets must therefore be recreation. That means to me, the whole process must be spontaneous behavior, or more simply: doing what I want to do at the rate of speed I want to do it, and enjoying the process without having to race to accomplish it. So, obviously, I cannot take orders.

Another limit has to do with my self-definition — who I am and what I want to do with my time on earth and what impression I would like to leave as my mark. That is, of course, very complex, but I can somewhat sum it up. I want to make use of the energies I am offered by the earth in such a way that the earth and I are both ahead. I see a society that is not doing that, so I want to make that statement with my work. Therefore, my baskets must help me, practically or aesthetically (or both). And they must appear handmade.

So back to this basket, which holds so many ideas.

You will need:

#2 reed

Cut eight stakes 26 inches long.

Beginning with the center (Fig. 46), and, *twining*, weave a circle about four inches across. Then cut sixteen stakes 11 inches long and add one to each existing stake. Break down and weave another inch. Then cut thirty-two stakes about 10 inches long and add them, making pairs of stakes.

At this point I changed to all dyed-weavers and *three rod wale* and began upsetting the sides. After a while I changed to one natural and two dyed-weavers. Then I upsett the ends and switched to two natural-weavers and one dyed. Finally, I used all three natural-weavers.

The border was worked with the pairs of stakes. It is one round (Fig. 33) and three rounds (Fig. 34), but all four rounds were done from right to left.

IX Flat Reeఎ Baskets

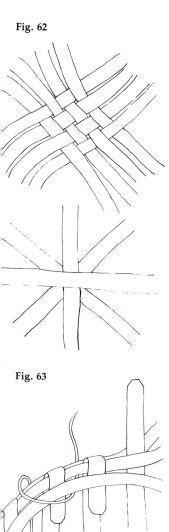

Fig. 62

Flat reed bottoms are generally one of two arrangements of stakes. The first is a square of the stakes woven together and the second a kind of star arrangement (Fig. 62).

Any weave can be used. It is the border that is very different from the type of baskets elsewhere in this book. The photo below illustrates one method, which I will explain. The carryall and the cat basket were done this way as well.

Flat reed border: You need three pieces of flat reed long enough to go around the top edge. The first one is used to bend the tops of the stakes over. The second goes around on the inside, the third on the outside. The stakes must be soaked and bent carefully. The pieces are bound together with a piece of cane, or twine as in Figure 63.

Binding on a flat reed border.

Fig. 63

The muffin basket shows an even easier way of disposing of the stake ends.

Muffin basket.

MUFFIN BASKET

This basket can almost be made just by looking at the picture. To me it is infinitely pleasing because it is so simple. Everything it does is right there. The bottom corners have a natural little bump to them.

You will need:

flat reed ½ inch
#2 reed

Cut eight pieces of flat reed 18 inches long. Weave these into a little square mat. Then weave *twining* weave, shaping gently up the sides.

The top edge is done by folding well-soaked stakes back on themselves and threading them down into the rows of weaving. To make them neat, I cut the ends off into a sort of blunt point.

This type of construction can be used on a larger scale to make scrap baskets and such.

CAT BASKET

I enjoyed this project but use the title wantonly, because just about any available basket is eventually appropriated by our cats.

This particular basket was made with folded newspaper for the stakes. I used one half of a full sheet, folded in half vertically, and folded in half again until it made a strip about an inch wide. You will need fourteen or sixteen such strips. It is woven with jute.

The center is actually a double bottom in this case because the newspaper stakes are so wide. This same center is often seen in Indian plaques forming the face of a kachina dancer. It can be done on a very small scale. Then the basket is woven with a lot of added stakes (Fig. 64). It is made by weaving back and forth in the center of half the stakes until a square shape of weaving has been done. Then another square is woven on the other stakes. Now lay one square on top of the other with the stakes lying in opposing directions. Tuck the ends of the weavers into the weaving unobtrusively. Then weave round and round. The basket will upsett itself as you weave unless you keep adding stakes, as illustrated in Figure 52.

Fig. 64

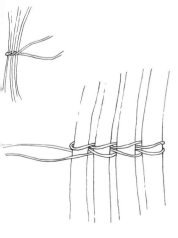

94

Twining weave is continued up the sides with random bits of color laid in. I wish I had made the sides higher.

For the top I folded the stakes back on themselves to the outside and tucked them into the weaving. Then I bound around a couple of times with jute threaded in a large needle.

Large carryall.

CARRYALL

My purpose was to make something the size of a grocery bag. I used narrow flat oval ¼-inch reed for some of the stakes and #6 half-round for the others. For a weaver, I used flat ¼-inch reed. There is no reason the stakes could not be all narrow flat oval, or ¼-inch flat reed.

The way I managed to shape this basket at all (for shaping

was the difficulty I had) was to fill a shopping bag with folded newspaper and use it as a mold. I bound the border on with some natural-colored jute, which I also used to weave the two handles. A small carryall appears on page 33.

I made the large carryall as big as I could to carry all my materials and to act as set dressing when I was weaving baskets in the window of Barclays Bank in Boston.

Bibliography

Allen, Elsie. *Pomo Basketmaking, a supreme art for the weaver.* Healdsburg, California: Naturegraph Publishers, 1972.

Bobart, H. H. *Basketwork Through the Ages.* London: Oxford University Press, 1950.

Boy Scouts of America. *Basketry.* North Brunswick, New Jersey, 1972.

Cary, Mara. *Basic Baskets.* Boston: Houghton Mifflin Company, 1975.

Crampton, Charles. *Canework.* Leicester, England: The Dryad Press, 1967.

Crampton, Charles. *The Junior Basket Maker.* Leicester, England: The Dryad Press, 1969.

Densmore, Francis. *How Indians Use Wild Plants for Food, Medicine and Crafts.* New York: Dover Publications, 1974.

Eaton, Allen. *Handicrafts of the Southern Highlands.* New York: Dover Publications, 1973.

Griswold, Lester and Kathleen. *The New Handicraft, Processes and Projects.* New York: Van Nostrand Reinhold Company, 1972.

Hart, Carol and Dan. *Natural Basketry.* New York: Watson-Guptill Publications, 1976.

Harvey, Virginia I. *The Techniques of Basketry.* New York: Van Nostrand Reinhold Company, 1974.

Hosking, Phyllis. *Basket Making for Amateurs.* London: G. Bell and Sons, Ltd., 1960.

James, George Wharton. *How to Make Baskets.* Glorietta, New Mexico: The Rio Grande Press, 1970.

————. *Indian Basketry.* Glorietta, New Mexico: The Rio Grande Press, 1970.

Ketchum, William C., Jr. *American Basketry and Woodenware.* New York: Macmillan Publishing Company, 1974.

Kronke, Grete. *Weaving With Cane and Reed.* New York: Van Nostrand Reinhold Company, 1968.

Lee, Martha L. *Basketry and Related Arts.* New York: D. Van Nostrand Company, 1948.

Leftwich, Rodney L. *Arts and Crafts of the Cherokee.* Cullowhee, North Carolina: Land-of-the-Sky Press, 1970.

Legg, Evelyn. *Adventure Into Basketry.* London: Mills and Boon Ltd., 1960.

McKee, Barbara, and Herold, Edwin and Joyce. *Havasupaï Baskets and Their Makers: 1930–1940.* North Flagstaff, Arizona: Northland Press, 1975.

Miles, Charles, and Bovis, Pierre. *American Indian and Eskimo Basketry, a Key to Identification.* New York: Bonanza Books, 1969.

Navajo School of Indian Basketry. *Indian Basket Weaving.* New York: Dover Publications, 1971.

Paul, Frances. *Spruce Root Basketry of the Alaskan Tlingit.* Lawrence, Kansas: Education Division, United States Indian Service, 1944.

Raycraft, Don and Carol. *Country Baskets.* Des Moines, Iowa: Wallace Homestead Book Company, 1976.

Rossbach, Ed. *Baskets as Textile Art.* New York: Van Nostrand Reinhold Company, 1973.

Rossbach, Ed. *The New Basketry.* New York: Van Nostrand Reinhold Company, 1976.

Schneider, Richard C. *Crafts of the North American Indian.* New York: Van Nostrand Reinhold, 1972.

Scott, O. R. *Basketry Step by Step.* London: Sir Isaac Pitman & Sons Ltd., 1958.

Seeler, Katherine and Edgar. *Nantucket Lightship Baskets.* Nantucket, Massachusetts: The Deermouse Press, 1972.

Sober, Marion Burr. *Basket Patterns.* Box 294, Plymouth, Michigan 48170, 1975.

Stephens, Cleo M. *Willow Spokes and Wickerwork.* Harrisburg, Pennsylvania: Stackpole Books, 1975.

Teleki, Gloria Roth. *The Baskets of Rural America.* New York: E. P. Dutton and Company, 1975.

Tod, Osma Gallinger, and Benson, Oscar H. *Weaving with Reeds and Fibers.* New York: Dover Publications, 1975.

Whitbourn, K. *Introducing Rushcraft.* Newton Centre, Massachusetts: Charles T. Branford Company, 1969.

Wright, Dorothy. *Baskets and Basketry.* Newton Centre, Massachusetts: Charles T. Branford Company, 1959.

Wright, Dorothy. *The Complete Guide to Basket Weaving.* New York: Drake Publishers, 1973.

Gallery of Baskets

I can't remember what kind of
vine this is. The larger basket is
about 10 inches across.

This is a sturdy little oval shopping basket that I use a lot. It is mostly of #4 reed. It is about 16 inches long and has a roped handle.

Twining with one #4 round reed
weaver and a narrow flat oval
weaver makes a distinctive
texture.

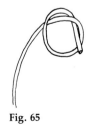

Fig. 65

This irresponsible little basket
illustrates how one can make a
chain of rings. See Figure 65.

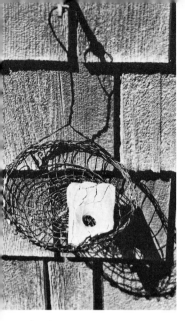

This far-out photo was taken by my husband. The wire rusted in no time once I started using the "basket." I used needle-nosed pliers to curl the ends of the stakes.

This is one of my "earliest works." I hang it on the Christmas tree.

Anything is possible, but it took a lot of trial and error to arrive at this "semblance" of a cornucopia.

An example of "trial and error" salvaged.

Our local hardware store had a special on this nice rope. I made a lot of things with it.

Rose hip cough syrup.

After I invented a beginning, I wove *double-twist* weave, using one weaver of linen twine and the other weaver of five pieces of #2 reed.

The inside story. This basket was hard to do, but I think it's really pretty. You can see that one stake broke. "Oh well!" I said and went on. The stakes are #6 reed. The basket measures about 18 inches across.

The rucksack that didn't do.

#4 reed working as a hot-plate mat.

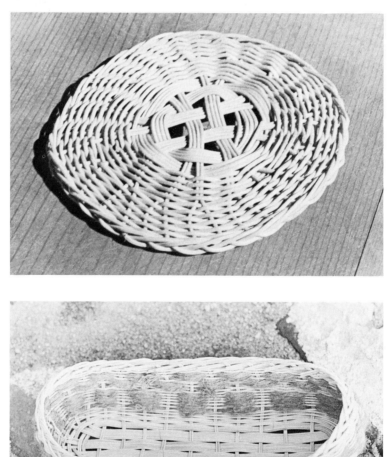

Here is an oval center I copied from a broken pocketbook.

This basket was made by Maida Fishman. She wasn't as pleased with it as I was and still am.

If you look very closely you can see a couple holding hands in the middle. I made this using #5 reed and raffia as a wedding present. It is amazingly strong.

This is a carryall I've used a lot.
The handle is finger weaving,
tied on. It is made with #5 reed
stakes. Flat reed is the weaver
on the sides.

Sometimes I just like to have
fun.

"Ever and still to Andy and
Bill."